B. Global Publishing and The Breathe Project Present

ONE AND DONE

The Korleone Young story as told To Kevin Harrison

By Kevin Sylvester Harrison, Ed.D and Korleone Young

One and Done
Copyright © 2020 by (Kevin Harrison & Korleone Young)

All rights reserved. No part of this book may be reproduced or transmitted in any form or by any means without written permission from the author.

ISBN (978-1-7360597-0-8)

Printed in USA by b.global publishing, One Umbrella, and The Breathe Project
Edited By Claudette L. Harrison
Cover Design by Riccardo Harris

Forward by Kevin Sylvester Harrison, Ed.D

•

It was roughly 3:50 AM on Monday, November, 21, 2016. I had yet to fully awaken. Most likely, I passed out watching television late Sunday night. I could faintly hear the phone ringing along with the voice of a television evangelist seeking donations. These noises seemed surreal as they dissolved into soundscapes of unconscious, yet lucid delusion. Moments later, the evangelist's voice grew distant, but the phone ringing swelled in intensity. Back-to-back calls, one after the next, fi ally startled me, so I rolled over slowly to answer the phone that had by this time stopped ringing. It took a few moments to bring my eyes into focus, but after doing so, I realized that Korleone had called me repeatedly, close to a dozen times. I knew that his mother, Kim, had been having some health issues, so my immediate concern was whether or not she was okay. I sat up and called him back immediately. He answered on the fi st ring, and though he was trying to speak, the combination of crying, screaming, and hyperventilating made his words sound cryptic and obscure.

Nonetheless, I didn't need to understand his words. From his emotion, I knew that his mother's health had likely taken a turn for the worst. Deep down and based on Korleone's erratic discourse, I knew that she had likely lost her ongoing battle with various medical conditions. Still I remained hopeful. I jumped up out of bed, quickly clothed myself, and rushed to his mother's apartment, which is roughly a five-minute drive from my house. When I arrived a little after 4:00 AM, I could hear Korleone crying from the hallway as I was walking up the stairs. His older cousin Antoine opened the door to greet me. Immediately, I saw Korleone's long frame extended across his mother's lifeless body, crying profusely and yelling "she's gone" at the top of his lungs. Minutes later, Antoine's brother, Deon, arrived with their mother, Korleone's late Aunt Beverly. A bit later, Deon and Antoine's other brother, and Beverly's middle son, Terry, arrived with his fiancé. It was a moment that seemed to stand still, as tears and hugs were exchanged throughout the room. I, too, watched with tear-filled eyes as Korleone's older cousins and aunt did their best to comfort him.

I'm ten years older than Korleone, and the two of us come from the same neighborhood. Therefore, I've known him most of his life. Our community was so close knit that many of the families functioned like extended relatives rather than neighbors; so in a sense, he is like a younger brother to me and some of the older boys from the block. I continued to watch him feeling helpless, crying uncontrollably while caressing his mother's body. Suddenly, I didn't see the 6'7" former professional basketball player who had been around the world and back. I didn't see a 37 year old whose life had modeled the lyrics to Marvin Gaye's "Trouble Man." I didn't see the man among boys who would dominate city league games as a standout player at Wichita High School East, nor did I see the 10th player in history to be drafted from high school to the NBA. Instead, I saw that little kid who grew up on 24th and Lorraine in Northeast Wichita, Kansas. I saw that little boy who would run in the house and tell his mother and grandparents when the older boys picked on him. I saw the tall kid who seemed to grow out of his school clothes twice each school year, but was so spoiled that he would have gotten new clothes regardless. I saw a kid who lived so close to me that you could see his porch from my backyard. Most of all, I saw a kid devastated by the reality that he would no longer get good morning calls, kisses on the cheek, and happy birthday wishes from the woman who had raised him – his loving mother Kimberly Young.

Korleone's life up to that point had been filled with both truimphs and disappointments, but I knew that nothing in the world mattered to him as much as his mother. He had made history by becoming the sixth McDonald's All-American to ever come from Wichita, Kansas; and one of few to skip college and be drafted to the NBA. Kim Young had been there to celebrate each of her son's accomplishments. Later in life, he had lost his career, been robbed at gunpoint, and shot at by two gunmen, and Kim was there to kiss away the pain just as she had done for bruises, scrapes, and cuts throughout his childhood. Th ough all of the peaks and valleys, no moment had been greater than being held in the loving grasp of Kim Young, and none more devastating than the moment I was witnessing as he fought to come to grips with the reality of her passing.

It was at this moment I knew that the Korleone Young story needed to be completed. He and I had gone back and forth for several years discussing the book, and at times we would complete a chapter here or a few paragraphs there. We would argue, fuss, and occassionally even wrestle with one another as means of expressing our frustrations and disagreements on everything from the direction the story should go, to what content to include or exclude, and even the number of pages and chapters. Sometimes he was excited about working and I would check out; other times, I would get excited and he would check out. Th s time, there would be no checking out.

I don't know that this was the best time to have this conversation with Korleone, but I pulled him away from his family during their mourning and whispered these words:

> Man, we have no choice bro. We've got to to fin sh your book, and we've got to make it impactful. Your legacy is a part of your mother's legacy, and it is up to you to carry her legacy on through your works and deeds. Most importantly, we can touch so many lives through sharing the highs and lows of your life. Don't spend too much time thinking about it today, but when you get yourself together, let's rap. But we have to be honest, transparant, and vulnerable. I love you bro… I'll call you and check on you after work.

While at work, I received a text message from Korleone that simply stated, "I'm ready." From that day forward, we have attempted to tap into his deepest emotions, face his most pressing fears, and expose his insecurities. It hasn't been an easy journey, but for both of us, it has been therapeutic. For Korleone, it has also been the release that he needed to face some of the realities that he has for so long avoided.

We hope you enjoy this journey! It is a journey of a young man who, from the outside looking in, always appeared to move through life's obstacles with the same ease that he had maneuvered through basketball defenders in highschool, AAU, and overseas. In actuality, like most us, his external shell failed to reveal the true butterfly beneath the cocoon. The façade of self-confide e and astuteness and the machismo disguise of a large muscular frame and aggressive highlight reels masked the true persona of a generous soul who cries, hurts, and feels. He forgives and seeks forgiveness; loves and seeks to be loved; and at this juncture of life, begins to pick up the broken fragments and start building a new legacy.

Some may have assumed that the Korleone Young story ended the moment he was cut from the NBA, but I am here to tell you over 20 years later that this story has just begun. Perhaps you've met the basketball superstar or the NBA hopeful that didn't quite make good, but until you've met the man, you have not met Korleone. Ladies and gentlemen, it is my pleasure to present to some and introduce to others, my good friend and my brother… Suntino Korelone Young. We hope that you enjoy!

Kevin Sylvester Harrison
Kevin Sylvester Harrison Ed.D

One and Done – The Korleone Young Story
(as told to Dr. Kevin Sylvester Harrison)
B. Global
The Breathe Project
2020 – All Rights Reserved

Dedicated in Loving Memory of Kim E. Young
March 19, 1957 – November 21, 2016
I Will Always Love you Mama

Contents

Forward by Kevin Sylvester Harrison, Ed.D iii
INTRODUCTION 1
CHAPTER 1: One and Done 7
CHAPTER 2: Family Values 16
CHAPTER 3: Tale of Two Fathers 25
CHAPTER 4: Robinson Middle School
             – Coach Randy Jackson 36
CHAPTER 5: Headed to High School – Rites of Passage 44
CHAPTER 6: East High Blue Aces 55
CHAPTER 7: Hargrave Military Academy 63
CHAPTER 8: AAU BASKETBALL 73
CHAPTER 9: Michael Jordan Flight School 85
CHAPTER 10: Mere Child's Play 92
CHAPTER 11: The Tale of Two Draft ights 105
CHAPTER 12: NBA: The Rookie 112
CHAPTER 13: The Legends 129

CHAPTER 14: A Dream Deferred 139

CHAPTER 15: Sweet Psalms in the Hour of Chaos 147

CHAPTER 16: Welcome to the Ghetto 155

CHAPTER 17: Arc of Redemption – Part One 165

CHAPTER 18: Arc of Redemption – Part Two Companion
 Guide and Summary 175

INTRODUCTION

●

Some critics suggest that I am the sole reason for the "One and Done" rule that currently requires prep basketball players to participate in one year of college basketball prior to entering the NBA draft. I've even heard the rule unofficially referred to as "The Korleone Young Rule." My name has become synonymous with a great deal of the ridicule that accompanies the prep-to-pro athletes who failed to become successful NBA professionals. Along with this ridicule are theories on things I should have, would have, and could have done differently. Some of what has been said is merely a pool of speculative rumors; however, some of it is at least partially true.

Part of the purpose for this book is to take control of the narrative. I figure who better to tell a story about Korleone Young than Korleone Young himself. It is my hope that through my story, kids and adults alike can become inspired to believe that any dream is possible through diligence, hard work, faith, determination, and perseverance. Whether it is a young prospective athlete who benefits from my mistakes, or a kid with a gift for math and science desiring to turn pro in life not necessarily sports, I believe that my story has valuable life lessons; and I would like to pass those lessons on to help others become the absolute best person that they can be.

Additionally, my story is about redemption. Like the fi tional heavyweight boxer "Rocky" played by Sylvester Stallone, I want to show that getting knocked down is not the end, but a necessary step in any signifi ant journey. As long as you have one more "get up" than you have falls, you will be successful.

I hope to inspire you to have the audacity to dream big. Who would have thought that a kid from Wichita, Kansas would become the tenth high school athlete in history to be drafted to the NBA? I am a living witness that through hard work and faith in God, anything is possible. I am also an example that when we take our blessings for granted, they can be swept from beneath our feet.

Though I am an athlete, the highs and lows that I've experienced in athletics are common in many facets of life. I hope to inspire others to use my mistakes as learning tools to ignite greatness within themselves in sports, school, business, and beyond. More importantly, I want to take what I've learned from both my mistakes and successes and share these as tools for overcoming adversity, making positive life changes, and being the signifi ant life force that God has intended of us.

Hello, my name is Korleone Young, and this is my story. Welcome to "One and Done."

A dream doesn't become reality through magic; it takes sweat, determination and hard work.

Colin Powell

Me and Grandpa Young

CHAPTER 1

•

One and Done

Like most kids, I grew up with dreams and high hopes of everyone knowing my name and celebrating my accomplishments. I thought for certain that I would one day come back to my old neighborhood and give back to the community that had initially given so much to me, while being celebrated as "the one who made it." Honestly, it wasn't until middle school that I decided that basketball would be my ticket to wealth and stardom. Previously, I explored a variety of interests including bowling, football, soccer, and even ballet and tap dancing until finally realizing that I possessed certain skills and physical characteristics that made basketball the obvious choice.

I was always bigger and taller than kids my age. So imagine how corny I must have looked at five years old in leotards, standing a complete foot taller than the other kids in the dance class. Besides that, imagine the ridicule I received from older male cousins who were already active in sports. It was around the age of eleven that I would forever trade in my soft slippers and leotards for sneakers and gym shorts.

From then on, basketball has been a part of my life, and in some shape or form, will always be.

Far different from what I had envisioned, my dream of becoming famous came partially true. I became a household name, but not so much for international acclaim or celebrity achievement. Unlike the stories of the late Kobe Bryant and LeBron James, my story doesn't travel the pathway of millions of dollars, endorsement deals, and championship rings. Instead, I would become the poster child for arguments against kids making the jump from high school to the NBA.

Prior to the 1998 NBA draft, there had been seven individuals who had taken this career path. In 1998, I was one of three additional high school players to make this transition. The other two high school athletes drafted during my draft class were Rashard Lewis and Al Harrington, both of whom have enjoyed outstanding and lasting NBA careers. During my senior year of high school, I had the opportunity to play against both individuals and fared quite well. Some spectators even suggested that I was dominant in these games.

I played against Rashard in Lawrence, Kansas at the legendary Allen Fieldhouse, just two hours from my home in Wichita, KS. Rashard was quite the physical specimen, standing at 6'10", possessing size and strength that made him effective in the post, along with shooting and ball handling ability that made him equally fie ce on the perimeter. I had primarily spent my prep career playing in the post with my back to the rim, so with Rashard I would be giving up three inches in addition to having to compete with his versatility and ability to play multiple positions on the court, offensively and defensively. I can honestly say that as an athlete, this kid was a freak of nature unlike anything I had seen up to that point. Nonetheless, I've never been one to back down from a challenge, so I was quick to embrace the opportunity to compete against the best of the best. In addition to leading my team to victory with over 20 points and double-digit rebounds, I displayed an assortment of monster dunks that left the crowd in awe. One spectator was Eric Bossi, who currently serves as a national recruiting analyst for Rivals.com. In a tweet dated May 28, 2014, Bossi went on record recalling the game, saying that I had dunked so many times on Rashard that he had to be taken out of the game crying:

Eric Bossi
@ebosshoops

Around this time 18 years ago, I once saw Korleone Young dunk on Rashard Lewis so many times, Lewis had to be taken out of game crying.

10:05 PM · May 28, 2014 · TweetDeck

I played against Al Harrington in one of the most historically signifi ant basketball arenas in America, the legendary Madison Square Garden. Al is a native of nearby Orange, New Jersey, so a packed house was in attendance to see the All-American product of the renowned powerhouse St. Patrick High School. Th s wasn't the fi st time the two of us had been opponents. We had met on the AAU circuit on one previous occasion in Washington, D.C. In the D.C. game, I led my Children's Mercy Hospital (CMH) team to victory over Al's New Jersey Road Runner squad to reach the tournament championship. We ended up losing the fi al game to a loaded Riverside Church team which featured future NBA stars Elton Brand and Ron Artest. In each game against Harrington, I scored more than 20 points, and in the Garden

(Madison Square Garden), I celebrated one of my most crowning high school accomplishments. Although Al had a great game as well, I guided my team, Hargrave Academy, to a four-point victory and solidifi d my place as one of the nation's elite college recruits. Th oughout the season, Al and I went back and forth fi hting for the top player in the country honor, so high stakes were on the line, as college coaches and NBA scouts were both in attendance.

Al and I exchanged blows like two heavyweight fi hters. Dunks, long range jump shots, and a heavy dose of smack talking ensued from start to fin sh. Late in the fourth quarter I fouled out, but remained effective as the emotional leader of my team. I am thankful for the rigorous academic requirements at Hargrave, which gave me access to language and references that I was previously unaccustomed to. During a time-out, I quoted part of a passage from William Ernest Henley's "Invictus" to ensure my team that as long as we had one another, we had nothing to fear. With just under two-and-a-half minutes remaining in the game, my teammate, Lavar Hemphill, went out and nailed a clutch three point shot to break a 56-56 tie game. We had trailed the entire game up to that point, so this momentum shift was exactly what we needed. A few solid defensive plays later and we were soon celebrating a 63-59 victory.

Both Rashard and Al have since retired from the NBA after enjoying lucrative careers that have grossed each of them over $100 million in career earnings. The decision to skip college and become professionals worked out quite well for both of them, despite the criticism that all three of us faced when such decisions were made. For me, on the other hand, the story turned out drastically different. I wouldn't like to think that I proved the critics right, but my misfortune has been used as one of the primary arguments in favor of the NBA "One and Done" ruling, implemented in 2005. Th s is the rule that makes it mandatory for prospective athletes to attend one year of college prior to being eligible for the NBA draft. Except for the select few athletes who opt to skip college and play overseas immediately following the end of their high school career, almost every elite prospect must attend one year of college before becoming NBA draft ligible.

From 2003 to 2005, 22 high school seniors opted to skip college and pursue NBA careers. Dwight Howard, Josh Smith and Monta Ellis are among the names of some who have done well, while others haven't been as successful - some far less successful than I.

The thing to keep in mind is that just like the NBA, college basketball is big business, and the desire to circumvent the traditional college route had begun to somewhat diminish the talent pool that maintains this big business machine. Th s is a machine that rakes in over $1 billion dollars in revenue during its March Madness Tournament alone, and affords its premier coaches' luxuries, salaries, and endorsement deals that rival those of professional coaches and rock stars. Therefore, I seriously doubt that I am the sole reason for the "One and Done" ruling, but I will admit that I do play a role in the series of events leading to the ruling.

The greatest dream in my life was to one day play in the NBA. What I never imagined happening was that this dream would last for just one brief season - fewer than fi een total minutes of playing time to be precise. Playing one year and being done was never what the "One and Done" rule meant, but in a sense I guess you could say that I gave an alternate meaning to the term. Despite a short-lived NBA career, I enjoyed a wonderful professional career overseas, playing in several countries on multiple continents, allowing me to learn the game on a global stage, and learn life from the perspective of a global citizen.

As a professional athlete, I was fortunate to earn hundreds of thousands of dollars playing a game that I love, so the game treated me well despite not enjoying a lucrative NBA career. After playing two years in Russia, five years in China, one-year in Australia and less than one year in Israel, my career average as an international basketball player was just under 30 points per game. By most accounts, this would be considered highly successful. However, there is nothing that compares to playing at home in front of family and friends. Nothing in the world can replace that feeling.

Nonetheless, I feel that my life has been truly blessed. Do I have regrets or wish that things turned out differently? Of course I would like to have had a better career. I know without a doubt that I possessed the talent to do so. However, what is far more important than fortune and fame is that we learn from our mistakes and use those lessons to inspire, challenge, and uplift thers.

Turn with me through the pages of my life. Join me in celebrating my triumphs and cry with me as we share my shortcomings. More importantly, take time to refl ct on your own life and use my story as a source of inspiration to dream, overcome obstacles, and to have the courage to re-invent one's self and start over when necessary. Let's face our fears together while we make the next chapter our best chapter yet. Are you up for the challenge? I knew you would be… let's go out into this world and be great together.

One Love...

One heart...

Let's get together and be alright

Bob Marley

CHAPTER 2

•

Family Values

Other than a strong relationship with God, I can't think of anything more powerful than strong family values. Over my life, I've met many people who haven't experienced the luxury of a great family, so I defin tely view this as a blessing. Although my family wasn't one that resembled the traditional structure, there was never a time that I didn't feel loved and supported. I never had much of a relationship with my biological father, and still don't to this day, but I don't feel slighted at all. I've always been surrounded by so much love that I never had much of a chance to miss him. We have since developed a cordial relationship, which I will share more about later. Meanwhile, when I talk about family, he usually isn't in the equation. On the other hand, his parents (my grandparents) always reached out to me and were very supportive and loving.

The catalyst of our family was Charles Young, my maternal grandfather and personal superhero. In order to truly understand me, it takes understanding my grandfather. Th s isn't to suggest that I am even half the man that he was, but I do believe I share his compassion for others. Standing at 6'4" tall and a former professional basketball player himself with the Harlem Globetrotters, he was the most caring and gentle person one could ever imagine. He moved to Cushing, Oklahoma from Brooksville, Oklahoma during his 8th grade school year where he would meet my grandmother, Betty Brown.

My grandmother had polio throughout most of her childhood, so she was often forced to miss several weeks and even months of school. When she could attend school, she was subjected to a wheelchair and could very rarely play in the same manner as other kids her age. Due to her physical impairments, she was typically overlooked by male classmates. My grandfather, on the other hand, looked beyond her physical imperfections and saw my grandmother for the beautiful soul that she was. In fact, my grandfather is the only man my grandmother ever dated.

I may be guilty of a lot of things, but hurting others is never something that I do intentionally. In fact, I have primarily caused more harm to myself than to others. As far as others are concerned, I'm a lot like my grandfather for the simple fact that I look beyond the external imperfections of others and try to see the beauty that resides within them. Most of my friends will agree with this statement. I never resented my biological father for his lack of involvement in my life, and when I was fi ancially capable, I gave him money a time or two. Th s is just the way that Grandpa Young taught me to be, and these values are so deeply instilled in me that I cannot express hatred or envy even when I try to.

During the era of my grandparents' teenage years, it was common for families to pick cotton to make ends meet. The fact that my grandfather was an exceptional athlete typically exempted him from such tedious work. My grandmother should have been exempt due to her sickness, but she chose to be out in the fi lds with her grandmother regardless. By the time she was 14, she had already endured multiple experimental surgeries and was often crippled or in pain.

I'm not totally familiar with how cotton-picking works, but from what I was told, there was some type of wheel-pulled contraption that my grandmother would sit in, and her siblings would push her up ahead. Grandma would pick cotton by herself in the front of the pack until everyone else caught up then they would push her up ahead again to repeat the process. There were even times when my grandmother would go out and pick cotton while out of school due to her illness.

I believe that my work ethic comes from my grandmother. There are numerous rumors regarding my short stay in the NBA. I've even heard that work ethic was a factor. I want to go on record and say this. Th oughout my basketball career from biddy to the NBA, I have come across kids who were more athletic than I was, kids who were better shooters, kids with better footwork, and even kids who were bigger and stronger. What I haven't found even to this day are kids who work harder than I am willing to work. I currently train a group of high school and college players ranging in age from 17 to 20, and every single one of them will tell you that at 40 plus years old, none of them can outwork me in the gym.

My mother and I lived in a modest home in Northeast Wichita, along with my grandparents. I am my mom's only child, but I do have two siblings from my biological father, a brother and a sister. I love my siblings but have never spent enough time around them to have any type of real relationship. However, I never grew up like an only child. In fact, my extended family was so close knit that we operated like a small village.

My Aunt Kathy and her two sons, Brandon and Cody, were with us in everything we ever did. They didn't live with us but spent so much time around us that Brandon and Cody were much more like brothers than cousins. We did all the things together that three brothers would do, including everything from learning to ride bicycles to walking through the house and past the restroom to go outside and pee in the backyard. Boys will always be boys, and we were no exception to that rule. We were rough, rugged, active, and mischievous like most boys.

I was the oldest, so I was extremely overprotective of my two younger "brothers", but whenever we did have an altercation as brothers sometimes do, I must honestly say that every battle was a close call. Afterwards, we never held any grudges and went right back to playing together as if nothing had happened.

I've always been considered tall, but height must be something that runs in our family. Standing at 6'7" tall, Brandon has enjoyed a lucrative long-term career playing professional basketball overseas. I love that the game has awarded Brandon the life of an international citizen, living on various continents, learning different customs, and broadening his perspective of the world. Cody is taller than both of us, standing at 6'8" and honestly, was naturally the best shooter of all of us. The funny thing about Cody is that he never really had any passion for the game, and by high school had become disinterested in continuing to play. As a kid, I never understood why he wouldn't play but as I have gotten older, I respect his decision tremendously. With his height and natural ability, school coaches drooled over Cody; yet at 17 years old, he had the leadership capacity to make his own decision and walk away from basketball completely.

I don't think two sisters could have been any closer than Mom and Aunt Kathy, as they were practically inseparable. Mom was barely a year older, yet the two were often mistaken for twins. Both were highly protective of one another. Rumor has it that during their younger years, if you fought one you had to fi ht the other. Everyone who remembers them swears that they were undefeated even when the opponents were male.

As tough as Mom was, she was never tough on me. Aunt Kathy, along with most of my cousins swore that I was spoiled rotten. I can't help but laugh when I think about denying how spoiled I was, when it was 100% true. As far as Kim Young was concerned, I could do no wrong. Damn, I miss my mama! She passed away in 2016, and a part of me passed away as well. My hope is that through rewriting the story of my own life, her legacy will continue to shine through my good works.

My grandparents are now deceased as well. Dealing with loss is something I have always had trouble with, but each day I get stronger and cope a little better than the day before. Despite learning to cope, it still causes depression from time to time. Having to come to grips with the fact that God doesn't provide us the luxury of keeping our loved ones forever is a reality that we all have to face, and I realize that we are taught not to question Him, but often, while crying myself to sleep at night, I can't help but ask God "Why?"

There was also the depression of not lasting in the NBA. Then there was a seven-figu e bank account that disappeared as quickly as my NBA career, coupled with the embarrassment of coming home to friends and family and having to answer tough questions that I honestly didn't know the answer to. Quite a bit of pressure for a kid who was just beginning to explore adulthood.

My coping mechanisms have not always been synonymous with positive lifestyle choices. I once heard Oprah Winfrey speak about people who have been hurt, becoming damaged, then unknowingly and unintentionally transferring that pain to others. At times, I have resorted to excessive use of alcohol and marijuana as means of coping, as well as engaging in promiscuity and womanizing. There have even been times that I wasn't the best father, son, grandson, or even friend in some cases. I started my journey with the intention of saving my community, but ultimately had become so burdened by my own demons that I was incapable of saving myself. To any persons whom I have offended, I am sincerely and truly sorry!

Brandon Korleone Cody

I'm from 24th and Hillside on the

Northside, down the street from

Popeyes, a Ninety-Eight Olds is what I

used to drive. Round the way from

St. Mark C-O-G-I-C, reminiscing when

It was Club Celebrities...

Lyrics from "I Put that on My Daughter, by Kevin S. Harrison

CHAPTER 3

•

Tale of Two Fathers

He passed away and I didn't cry, 'cause my anger, wouldn't let me feel for a stranger...

Tupac Shakur

Father One: Juan Johnson

In the song "Dear Mama," Tupac Shakur references viewing his deceased biological father lying in a casket, yet not feeling any pain about the situation. Although my father is still alive, I can certainly relate to Shakur's sentiment of having no relationship with his dad. Several of my friends enjoyed bonding with their fathers, playing catch in the backyard, sharing in life lessons, and engaging in various rites of passage that accompany manhood. I never experienced such good fortune, and though I would be lying if I said I didn't want it from time to time, I never felt as if I lacked any of the socio-emotional development that comes from a healthy father-son relationship.

I never had enough exposure to my father to gauge whether I respected him or not, but if there were ever any discontent in my heart, it dissolved on November 26, 2016. Th s was the day of my mother's funeral service. Having endured more than his fair share of health concerns, he stood up slowly, and sluggishly approached the podium to make remarks. I was nervous and even angry contemplating what he may or may not say. Bent over and using the assistance of a walking cane, he continued to slowly approach the microphone. I'm sure it couldn't have taken longer than a minute or so, but anxiety and nervous energy seemed to pause time as his approach seemed endless. He fi ally reached the podium microphone and slowly uttered thoughtful words that would change my impression of him forever.

In a crackling tone, with volume fading and swelling, he was at times hard to hear, yet his message quite powerful. Inside a small mortuary packed to capacity with over 200 people crowded elbow to elbow, he gradually pulled a small crumply sheet of paper from his right hip pocket and began reading a message prewritten solely for comforting me during the toughest loss I had ever endured. He started by apologizing for failing to take active participation in my upbringing and fin shed with words of uplift and spiritual inspiration. Without question, I can certainly say that I wasn't expecting it, but surprisingly enough – I appreciated every word!

> *Korleone, I know I haven't been there for you*
> *like I should have been, or much at all for*
> *that matter over all these years.*

He paused to wipe his eyes and nose, sniffled, then continued speaking slowly and intentionally while everyone in attendance clung to his every word.

> *And I don't blame you if you don't ever want to*
> *have anything to do with me. No son, I*
> *really don't blame you. Not at all.*

He paused again while gathering his words, squinting at his paper, and nervously fid eted around his facial area. There was a moment of awkward silence, then he resumed speaking softly and as slowly as before, yet sincerely and with purpose.

> *I just want to say that I'm sorry for not being*
> *there, and Korelone, though I haven't been the*
> *best father, I want you to know that I love you*
> *and both of your grandparents… my parents…*
> *the Johnsons love you too. If there is anything*
> *that we can do for you, please, please, please, let us know!*

After another long pause, he brought his thoughts to a close saying,

> *Your mother did a great job raising you even though I wasn't there, and I just want you to know that God doesn't make mistakes and you'll see your mother again. I love you son!*

By this time, water is pouring from his eyes profusely. I remember trying hard to refrain from crying - trying to be hard and tough – trying to pretend that his words didn't touch me, but within seconds I broke down crying as well. Though a complete stranger for the most part, we seemed to have bonded. For the fi st time in my life, Juan Johnson was my father, and like a five-year-old excited to see his pops return home from work, I was that little bright-eyed boy sharing a special moment with his daddy.

Juan Johnson

Took me from a boy to a man so
I always had a father when my
biological didn't bother

                              Shaquille O'Neal

Father Two: Henry Jackson (aka Big Henry)

Since I am a former professional basketball player, I figued it would be appropriate to quote Shaquille O'Neal. He was perhaps the most dominant player that I have ever witnessed, but that's not as signifi ant for me as lyrics to his song "Biological Didn't Bother." The song itself is a tribute and dedication to a man named Philip Harrison. Sure, Shaq is known more for making dunks than he is for making music, but the song was extremely heartfelt. In the lyrics he expresses his admiration and respect for Harrison for providing a shining example of manhood in the absence of his biological father, thus the hook "He's my father 'cause my biological didn't bother." Like O'Neal, I too had a father figue who filled the void left vacant by my biological father. His name was Henry Jackson, but everyone who knew him affectionately called him Big Henry.

Big Henry started dated my mother when I was 11 or 12-years-old and had been a solid influence in my life from our initial meeting up to his time of death. I was playing professional basketball in Russia when I got the news that he had passed away, and I became immediately consumed with a wide range of thoughts and emotions. It wasn't too long after his return from prison for murder that he and my mother became an item, and he immediately became actively involved in my life.

I don't know all the details of the incident that landed him in prison, but the circles of influence are close knit in Wichita, so I have heard multiple rumors over the years. As a young and impressionable kid, I would be lying if I were to say that I didn't allow some of these rumors to shape my impression of Big Henry initially. However, the only thing I can base my judgement on is how he treated my mother and how he influenced my life, and in those capacities, he was an exemplary example of compassion, guidance, and love.

For those who didn't know him, his appearance alone could be intimidating. He was a wide framed man who stood just over six feet tall and weighed well over 300 pounds, with hands as hard as steel and the widest fi gers I've ever seen. He certainly looked about as dangerous as anyone I have ever encountered. However, once you got to know him, Big Henry was a sensitive soul with a heart of gold. I would go as far as calling him a gentle giant!

I remember getting the call from my mother that he had passed. They were no longer together, but she loved him deeply and was severely wounded by his passing, and quite frankly, so was I. For hours, I sat in my apartment in an unfamiliar country alone and sad, thinking of everything that I wish I had said to him while he was alive. "You ain't my daddy!" I would often blurt out whenever he would offer advice or demand that I speak respectfully when addressing my mother. Perhaps I was upset that my biological was never around or perhaps I had allowed the negative talk about Big Henry to affect my opinion. I'm not sure what it was, but I knew I was crying profusely, wishing the two of us could have just one more conversation. As I sat thinking about all the times I had rudely reminded him that he wasn't my father, I realized that he had been everything that I needed in a father figu e despite what others had said about him. If the opportunity were to present itself now, I would be proud to call him "dad", but one of my biggest regrets in life is that I will never get that opportunity.

As much as I pretended to ignore the life lessons stressed by Jackson, I secretly clung to every word. In sports and in life off the court, the voice of Big Henry has always played in my mind and still does, reminding me to work hard, respect others, and never give up on myself. The irony in all of this is that I see a strange similarity between my life and the life of Big Henry. So many were so quick to judge him based on his physical stature and an incident that they knew very little about. I've never spent time in prison, but I know what it feels like when others tell your story. Fortunately, Big Henry taught me how to deal with such skepticism. Though certain criticism is hurtful at times, like Big Henry, I am built to overcome tough circumstances. While my opportunity to tell him that I love him and miss him has come and gone, my opportunity to become the best person that I can be remains. The opportunity to pick up the broken pieces of my life and use my mistakes as life lessons for others still lies ahead of me. Not only do I have the opportunity to live a life with purpose and accountability, I also have the opportunity to continue the legacy of Big Henry in the same manner as his biological children. I often look in the mirror and motivate myself by saying "I am Big Henry" as a means of challenging myself to reach my goals. I know that if I accomplish greatness, I can stand as a shining example of his legacy by presenting to others the traits that he has instilled in me. To Hank, Greg, and Sunny, I thank you for sharing your father with me. Without him, I would've missed out on the mentorship that I foolishly took for granted.

Big Henry, I love you and I miss you big fella!

Wichita State University's Memorial '70

CHAPTER 4

•

Robinson Middle School – Coach Randy Jackson

My middle school basketball experience was unique. At the time, there were no female basketball programs in Wichita public middle schools. My girlfriend at the time was Latoya (Toya) Jackson, perhaps the best female player in the city for her age. Toya had dominated Biddy Basketball and tournament play and was about to make history as the fi st girl to compete on an all-boys team.

Toya quickly proved to be one of the most talented guards in the city as the only female player in the league, and I was regarded as one of the brightest prospects in league history. Th s means a lot considering that our coach, the late Randy Jackson (no relation to Toya) has coached a host of outstanding athletes. A couple of notable alums from Coach Jackson's Robinson teams include NCAA champion Clint Normore and NBA veteran player and world champion coach Adrian Griffi

Coach Jackson was a large, muscular, no-nonsense type of man who had played running back in the NFL for the Buff lo Bills, San

Francisco 49ers, and Philadelphia Eagles. Prior to a successful career as a professional athlete, he survived a tragic airplane crash that took place on October 2, 1970. As a member of the Wichita State University football team, Coach Jackson was on a fli ht headed to Utah for a game against Utah State. The game was never played, as one of the two planes transporting the Wichita State University team crashed into a mountain in Clear Creek County, Colorado, 40 miles West of Denver.

Thi ty-one people died, including 14 players, and an assortment of team staff, boosters, and fli ht crew members. Coach Jackson was one of only a handful of survivors including eight other players and a co-pilot. Rather than leaving and starting over elsewhere, he remained with the Wichita State University football team, going on to rush for eight touchdowns and close to 1000 yards the season following the tragedy.

I can't pretend to imagine the ongoing trauma that Coach Jackson might have experienced from this horrific and unpleasant incident. At the tender age of 21-years-old, he was just getting accustomed to adulthood and would have to relive this memory for the remainder of his days. His choice to return to Wichita State is a testament to his tenacity and resilience. It was in this same tenacious manner that he managed our basketball team at Robinson Middle School, and for a spoiled mama's boy like myself, man was it intense and tough!

Never one for excuses, he had no problem pushing me and my teammates harder than we were accustomed. His coaching philosophy was simple for the most part - run! Th s meant that we ran when we got in trouble and ran when we weren't in trouble; we ran in practice and we ran in games; and whenever there was nothing better to do, we ran. He let us know that he may not always have the most talented or most athletic team, but he would always have the best conditioned team.

With our team, Coach Jackson was fortunate to have the most athletic, most talented, and best conditioned team, featuring me, a future McDonald's All-American, and Toya, a girl who flat out gave boy players all they could handle. During my 8th grade year, we were undefeated, and I dominated the league in every statistical category. Despite being the best player in the city and averaging 33 points per game, Coach Jackson was probably harder on me than anyone else on the team. If I had 30 points and 20 rebounds, I should have had 35 and 25. Rather than celebrating 5 blocked shots, he would instead scrutinize me for missing opportunities to retain possession after the block. If I shot 90% from the free-throw line, I had to explain why I wasn't at 100%.

After dissecting every facet of my game, he had nothing left to analyze, so he came up with the Korleone dunk rule. Th s meant if I had a chance to dunk but settled for a lay-up, I had to run during the next practice. If a player had the opportunity to pass the ball to me for a dunk but settled for a lay-up, they had to run. If at any time the team missed an opportunity for my dunking the basketball, someone was going to be in trouble. At the time, I didn't realize the method to his madness, but he was preparing me to look beyond the physical activity of just scoring and focus on the mental component of intimidating and destroying opposing players. By the time I had reached high school, my size and strength increased, and my skillset grew exponentially, but my ability to intimidate opponents proved to be just as signifi ant as size and skill.

I lacked the maturity to appreciate it back then, but looking back on it, I see now why Coach Jackson seemed unusually tough on middle school boys. In addition to teaching physical education, he was also teaching manhood, accountability, and hard work. He simply wanted us to demand the best of ourselves, so he pushed us to see in ourselves what we may not have known was there. His military style of coaching would prove benefic al, and soon after, I began dominating at the high school level.

I will always look up to Coach Jackson as a mentor and a friend, and for being a signifi ant part of my growth and development as a player and as a person. I will forever admire his loyalty which he demonstrated not only by returning to Wichita State following the plane crash, but also by remaining a teacher and coach at the same school for over thirty years (Robinson); and remaining married and loyal to his wife Gail for thirty-four years.

On July 21, 2010, Coach Randy Jackson would turn in his coaching whistle for good, losing a hard fought battle to pancreatic cancer. If our lives are truly measured by the lives that we touch while on this earth, then Jackson is without question a shining example of stalwart leadership. I think I can speak for countless young men and women when I say that Coach Jackson touched a lot of lives over the course of a three decade career devoted to mentoring and challenging young people to pursue excellence. He certainly touched mine…

Coach Randy Jackson
November 13, 1948 – July 21, 2010

We must find time to stop and thank the
people who make a difference
in our lives....

                                        John F. Kennedy

When I was I child, I spoke as a child, I understood as a child, I thought as a child; but when I became a man, I put away childish things.

                                        1 Corinthians 13:11

CHAPTER 5

•

Headed to High School – Rites of Passage

A Rite of Passage is typically described as a ritual to celebrate an individual's advancement from one phase of life to the next. For example, the critical steps that accompany transitioning from boyhood to manhood would be considered Rites of Passage by some accounts. Th s notion is particularly true in sports. There are initiation steps that must be encountered as an athlete evolves, improves, and advances from one level of competition to the next. It is the obligation of tenured athletes to protect the integrity of competitive events by establishing barriers to entry designed to accommodate and accept only those who are prepared and equipped. Such challenges are as mentally tough as they are physical. Many talented athletes fail to overcome this potentially gruesome initiation process.

My Rite of Passage to high school was far tougher than what I had bargained for. It would require competing heads-up with the man that most consider the hands down best player to ever come out of Wichita, Kansas.

It happened the summer prior to my freshman year at Wichita High School East. Though nearly thirty years ago, I remember it like it was yesterday. My mom's boyfriend (Big Henry) decided that I needed to start playing pick-up games with grown men in order to toughen up for the upcoming high school season. These games proved to be some of the toughest and most intense battles imaginable. It was hard work, but I had the privilege of competing with several community and regional sports legends, including football Hall of Famer Barry Sanders, who is a phenomenal basketball player as well. During one such instance, I was on the same team with Steve Knighton, a member of the undefeated 1977 Wichita Heights High School Falcons team that many consider the best team in the history of Kansas high school basketball.

In addition to being coached by Lafayette Norwood, the first Black head coach of any sport in city league history, the team also featured two future McDonald's All-Americans, college All-Americans, and NBA draftees in Darnell Valentine and Antoine Carr. While Valentine and Carr were the focal points of the team, the squad was loaded with talent at every position. Many say that Knighton and a player named Calvin Alexander were the toughest and most physically dominant players in the city league during this era. Basketball heads in the community swear that it was the toughness of Knighton and Alexander that helped prepare the two superstars for successful college and professional careers.

Alexander went on to become a Golden Gloves Heavyweight champion and professional boxer, and still trains young fighters today. Knighton, still quite the basketball aficionado, is often seen at local high school games donning a sense of style and flair that many say is no different than how he presented himself as a high school student-athlete in 1977. I can't imagine a high school student in the late 70s wearing a bright colored suit and tie, accompanied by a matching wide-brimmed fedora and fluorescent alligator shoes, wrapped in a full-length mink coat, but everyone swears that Steve possessed the same flair in high school that he does today.

During the pick-up game with Knighton, I was assigned the task of guarding the most feared player to ever come out my hometown. A player so talented that he led Wichita South High School to three consecutive state titles in the late 1970s, while leading the city league in scoring his junior and senior seasons, averaging 27.1 and 31.7 respectively.

There have since been players who have rivaled these numbers, so to put a proper perspective on how legendary this player was, it is important to mention that other individuals mentioned in the same breath had the luxury of the three-point line, and four years of high school. There was no three-point line in high school basketball in the late 1970s. In fact, it wasn't until the 1979-1980 season that the NBA adopted the three-point shot. Plus, high school players typically played three years during this era rather than four.

Legend has it that this guy would take two to three steps across the half court line, let the ball fly, and many times turn his back on the shot and head back to play defense. I initially thought that stories about his shooting range were exaggerated, but on this day I would discover them to be true. I would go from being a fan of a legend I had heard about my entire life to being a terrifi d 14-year-old kid attempting to guard the man who in 1979 scored 41 points against Isiah Thomas in the Kansas-Illinois Classic. The man who in 1982, scored 20 points in leading his Tulsa Hurricane team to a 10-point defeat over a loaded North Carolina Tar Hills team that featured James Worthy, Sam Perkins, and freshman sensation Michael Jordan.

Ricky Ross (Tulsa) Vs. Michael Jordan (North Carolina)

The man I am talking about is none other than Ricky Ross. Ross lived up to every myth, running me around the court in a manner resembling Stephen Curry terrorizing defenders in the modern era. His shot was majestic, beautiful, and artistic. I was only 6'4" at the time, so at 6'6" he already had a slight height advantage. My assumption was that I would be able to leverage my wingspan and athleticism to contest his shots. To my surprise, he would fade away while still gaining altitude, almost defying gravity, making one shot after the next. Never as a player or spectator had I seen a player have the gall to shoot from 35 to 40 feet, yet Ross made these impossible shots appear as if he were shooting layups. Meanwhile, I chased around aimlessly trying to figure out the impossible task that many, including hall of famer Isiah Thomas, were incapable of accomplishing – successfully guarding Ricky Ross.

Though he only hit five shots with me guarding him, they came so quick and were so impressive that it felt like I had been guarding him for hours. The experience was exhausting and almost traumatizing. The entire time, Big Henry was yelling at me from the sidelines at the top of his lungs to the point that I felt as if I were being slightly bullied - not just by Big Henry, but by all parties in attendance. If I were going to be the best high school player in the city, the veterans were going to make me prove it right then and there. All eyes were on me and the pressure was at a blistering peak.

Finally, after Ross had scored another one of his signature and nearly impossible shots, Knighton threw me a baseball pass the length of the court. The ball carried so much velocity that it practically burned my fingers. Before I knew it, the ball was in my hands with nothing standing between me and the rim except Ross. Without thinking twice, I took one dribble and went airborne, colliding chest to chest with the legend, dunking so hard that I nearly pulled him through the rim along with the ball. Knighton immediately started screaming at the top of his lungs, "Yeeeeeaaahhhhhh young fella, that's what I'm talking about!!!

I could hear Big Henry screaming and yelling from the sidelines with equal enthusiasm. Everyone else in the gym became uncontrollable, as the sounds of the ball that I was still bouncing and my raging heartbeat were both drowned out by a chorus of taunting, laughter, and competitive banter. I could tell that Ross was slightly bothered as one would expect any great competitor to be, but he gave me my props. This was my rites of passage and what better way than having to go through one of the best in my town to ever do it.

The remainder of the summer, I continued to compete with older players. In many cases, guys were more athletic, more experienced, and even physically stronger than I was. My lanky frame and awkward build were still under development, and older and stronger opponents attempted to play physically and bully me around. I worked hard and competed with every breath and every drop of sweat, and continued to find ways to dominate the competition. Perhaps my most critical development was learning to mentally process the game and to out-think the opposition. In previous matchups, I had always been the biggest and strongest player on the court, so I could rely solely on size and strength. Now I was being tested like never before, and had to find other ways to be effective.

By the end of the summer, I had learned how to analyze player tendencies. Players who were stronger, forced me to learn how to use my speed and quickness; for quicker players, it taught me to leverage my length. For every strength a player possessed, I learned how to find a weakness that I could exploit and eventually defeat that opponent.

By the end of the summer, I had been battled-tested and was ready to begin my high school basketball career as a freshman at Wichita High School East. It had become crystal clear that Wichita High School basketball would be introducing a new sheriff, and his name was Korleone Young.

Wichita City League
All-City Selection - 1997

Wichita High School East

Why fit in when you were born
to stand out?

Dr. Seuss

Coach Ron Allen – Wichita High School East

CHAPTER 6

•

East High Blue Aces

I started high school in 1994. From the first time I walked the hallways of Wichita East to this very day, I literally get butterflies. A welcoming nostalgia dwells within the walls of the massive gothic structure that sits on an expansive 44-acre campus located just blocks east of downtown Wichita. Established in 1878 as Wichita High School, just 13 years after slavery was abolished, East High is the oldest high school in Wichita.

The current building was erected in 1928 and its walls echo the legendary whispers of the decades of students who have been privileged to occupy its hallways. From former Secretary of Defense Robert Gates, to legendary rock guitarist Joe Walsh of the Eagles, to civil rights activist Dr. Ronald Walters and countless others, there is something about East High that is synonymous with excellence.

Not only would I be wearing the same Blue Aces logo that was donned by the likes of world record setting mile runner Jim Ryan, NCAA basketball champion Clint Normore, and far too many others to list, I would also be tasked with the challenge of repeating what

Adrian Griffi had done two years prior to my arrival - win a state championship. Under the direction of legendary Coach Ron Allen, it was inevitable that we would make history.

Coach Allen was a player's coach who had been a star on both the high school and collegiate level, as a player and as an advocate for social justice. Legend has it that Coach was a stellar guard with the ability to slash through opposing defenders and shoot the ball lights out. As the fi st Black player in the history of Wichita Southeast, I imagine he became just as elusive at maneuvering through various racial obstacles as he was penetrating the defensive schemes of opposing teams. It was only fitting that Allen would fin sh his college career playing for Coach Fred Snowden and the Arizona Wildcats. In the same manner that Allen broke the color barrier at Wichita Southeast, Snowden broke the color barrier in coaching, becoming the fi st Black head coach of a major university.

Our team was loaded with talent, and by the time I had become a junior we were practically unbeatable. With the exception of two close games against Wichita Southeast, we started the season on fi e, defeating each opponent by a minimum of 15 points. Southeast was a talented team, led by the outstanding guard play of Tony Brown, a student one year my senior. After flat-out dogfi hts in both contests, and despite 20+ point performances by Brown in each, we managed to squeak by with three and four-point victories in each of those games.

With our second game against Wichita Heights on the horizon, we became complacent, and lost some of the fi e that had made us special. We had already beaten Heights by double digits at East, so winning the upcoming game in their gym would be the last game of the season and an exclamation point that would make us the fi st undefeated team since the 1988 South High team that featured future division one stars Val Barnes who became a star player for Iowa University, Steve Woodberry, who would become a star for the University of Kansas, and an extremely talented supporting cast of stellar players at every position, including my own cousin, Deon White. Th s was the fi st season that Heights former assistant coach Joe Auer would assume the head coaching position. Prior to serving as the head basketball coach, he served as the head baseball coach for Heights, and was responsible for 11 city league baseball titles. Auer has since gone on to make history in basketball as well, with an unprecedented run of four state championships from 2008 to 2012, and an additional state championship in 2015. However, this was a test that the up and coming coach should have been destined to fail.

Prior to the heavily anticipated season fi ale against Heights, we were scheduled to compete in a tournament in Topeka, Kansas, followed by another city league game, then the game that the entire city was waiting for – Wichita East vs. Wichita Heights. After spending three years as a standout athlete, it was fi ally my time to really shine. I was ready to make history by leading my team to an undefeated season, then go on to claim a state title. To my surprise and disappointment, my whole world was about to be shaken to pieces.

During my sophomore year, I had already been in trouble for taking part in a locker room initiation process that was mistaken for an altercation, during which time I was suspended for half a game. Th s time the stakes were higher as alcohol was involved and I was now a repeat offender. With my presence being the biggest in the city, it was time for an example to be made, and I would be the fall guy despite the involvement of several other students.

At the time, I felt targeted, but looking back at the incident as an adult, I understand exactly why the brunt fell squarely on my shoulders. Theodor Seuss Geisel (aka Dr. Seuss) sums it up best in a quote that says "Why fit in when you were born to stand out?" I was the most popular high school athlete in the state of Kansas; I had been ranked top five in the nation since my freshman year; and I was physically bigger than all of the other students. Therefore, I was designed for leadership both on and off the basketball court. However, instead of accepting my destiny to lead, demonstrate a positive example, and influence others to do the right thing, I made the poor choice of trying to "fit in."

I had several good friends who played on the basketball team, and several others who became yell leaders just so they could travel with the team. Team trips had become quite the party, and celebrations were often inappropriate in terms of how high school kids are expected to behave. Under-age drinking was typically one of many facets of our gross negligence and misconduct. It was on a Saturday night, and we had just won the tournament in Topeka, Kansas. Like most of our travel games, a group of affluent White kids comprised of cheerleaders and players brought alcohol on the trip. Close to a dozen of us gathered in the room of one of the cheerleaders and the drinking began.

After a couple of hours, one of the cheer coaches unexpectedly and abruptly entered the room to fi d it occupied by intoxicated minors. Coach Allen was contacted and soon after, what began as a celebration for winning a tough tournament, quickly turned into a chastising session. After a painful and humiliating lecture, everyone was sent to their respective rooms and given a strict curfew.

We returned to school on Monday expecting to deal with further repercussions, but hoping that the incident wouldn't be reported. Of course, we wouldn't be so lucky, and sure enough, while sitting in one of my morning classes, I heard the unpleasant sound of my name announced loudly over the school intercom. "Korleone Young, report to the offic " Immediately I felt a sickness in my stomach as I knew what was coming next. After a slow and painful walk down the hallway, I fi ally arrived at the school offic where the principal, Ms. McHenry awaited. Since she played college basketball, I thought that she would certainly give me a break. I briefly imagined us engaging in a laugh as she shared a story of something irresponsible from her past as a teaching lesson. My daydream was just getting good, when my overactive imagination was interrupted by the crude reality that I would be suspended for five games.

There were at least 12 students in the room, all intoxicated, yet I was solely chosen to take the fall. Was it fair? Probably not, and I quickly assumed the victim role as one would expect of a 17-year-old kid. The students who provided the liquor, the cheerleader whose room was invaded, and several other students had no consequence other than the lecture that took place at the Topeka Ramada. Now with an undefeated season on the line, I was forced to miss critical games, including the upcoming battle with rival competitor Heights High School. I sat at home sad, pondering the outcome as we lost the game. Much more signifi ant than this one game was that the dynamics of the team would drastically change. We were the top ranked team in the state and a heavy favorite to win the Kansas State Title, and though loaded with talent, we functioned in an unselfish manner prior to this point. We lost the Heights game by two points and the magic would never return.

Despite playing sloppily and selfishly, we were talented enough to advance throughout the state tournament until fi ally reaching the state semi-finals. This is where reality finally caught up with us. We lost the state semi-final by two points to a Kansas City area school, Olathe South. I was the emotional and physical leader of our team, and my actions sucked the heart and soul out of us, and in some ways out of our season.

While I blamed everyone except myself, the reality is that I have always known what is right from what is wrong. Was I treated unfairly due to my local celebrity status? Was I unfairly used as an example? Despite the answer to these questions, the lesson that I learned is worthy of sharing. Every action has an equal and opposite reaction is a law of physics that applies to everything we do in life. So despite others not receiving consequences, the fact remained that I was in control of my actions, and I was wrong.

A true test of leadership is doing the right thing even when it isn't popular to do so. I had every opportunity to act in a responsible manner and to influence the others to do the same; yet I neglected to do so. I let myself down, I let my school down and I let my team down. My challenge to you is to be better than me. My consequence of being suspended five games was devastating, but mild in comparison to countless numbers of young people who have lost their physical freedom and even their lives due to "fitting in" rather than "standing out" – following rather than a leading – making poor decisions rather than doing what is right.

I was hard on myself for the turn that our season took. I feel 100% confident to this day that had I not been suspended, we would have won state and enjoyed an undefeated season. Looking back through the eyes of a man approaching middle-age, I see it from a much clearer perspective.

After consulting with my mother and my AAU Coach Myron Piggie, we collectively agreed that my exposure had grown too large for Wichita. I had become such a phenome that I had potentially become a distraction, so I needed an atmosphere that would challenge me to focus on becoming a better player, a better student, and a better person. I needed a place where I would be far removed from the distractions that tempt young men to make poor choices. Everything I needed would soon be my reality. I transferred from Wichita East and spent my senior season at Hargrave Military Academy in the southern Virginia town of Chatham.

CHAPTER 7

•

Hargrave Military Academy

In terms of entertainment and social activity, there wasn't much to do in Chatham, Virginia. One grocery store, one gas station, and not a single traffic light occupied the small town of just under 1400 residents. Traveling the globe on the AAU (Amateur Athletic Union) basketball circuit allowed me to visit Kansas City, Las Vegas, Los Angeles, New York, and a host of other cities that made Wichita seem small. Suddenly, my hometown of just under 400,000 seemed enormous in comparison to Chatham.

The closest sign to anything resembling civilization was roughly 15 miles away from the Hargrave campus. I didn't have a car, so fifteen miles of dusty Virginia backroads felt as endless as a cross country road trip. On rare occasions, we took team trips into town, but even with the camaraderie of the entire team and coaching staff, I found these journeys terrifying. Rich forestry cast shadows of darkness on rigid dirt pavement, making it difficult to distinguish the darkest nights from the brightest days.

Based on the racial history of Chatham, I would often imagine the stories that would be told if these ancient trees could speak. Do these woods hold the secret whispers of slave lynching and vicious dog attacks? Did these forests witness passengers moving through unfamiliar terrain and dark Virginia nights via the underground-railroad? Is the soil of this earth moistened by the blood and tears of captured runaways? These are the types of questions I would often ask myself as a homesick teenager living in a strange environment, over 1000 miles from home. Being lonely and homesick, combined with additional racial fears was an overwhelming existence for a kid who had never been more than 20 miles away from his mother and grandparents.

Chatham is only 180 miles from Jamestown, Virginia, the alleged location where the nation's fi st slaves stepped onto North American soil in 1619. Locals swear that this may be the fi st date of legal slavery, but believe that Virginia slavery dates to the middle 1500s with the heart of tobacco slavery residing in nearby Danville County. I immediately went into depression. My fears of being away from home were compounded by the discomfort of residing in the shadows of trees that my ancestors likely hung from. Here I was a 6'7" seventeen-year-old with the muscular build of a twenty-four year old professional athlete, yet during my fi st week in Virginia, my massive frame spent as much time hovering over a payphone crying to the calming sound of my mother's voice as it did practicing post moves and free throws.

Thankfully, my AAU coach's son and teammate, Myron Piggie, Jr., enrolled with me, so I was never completely alone. Shortly thereafter, I met several of my teammates and classmates, and developed friendships that still exist today. Before long, I had accepted Hargrave Academy as the place that I would call home for my senior year of high school. I was far away from my friends, family, and the stardom I had experienced as the hometown superstar of Wichita, but I was ready for a brand new challenge, and ready to accept my teammates as my new extended family.

In many ways, it felt like starting over, but the people advising me thought that this was the best move based on a couple of factors. As previously stated, I had gotten into trouble on two separate occasions. The previously mentioned hazing and drinking incidents were both situations that involved several players, but in both cases I received the most severe punishment. At the time, I looked at this as being unfair, but looking back, I was the team leader. Anyone in a leadership role must understand that the expectations, the stakes, and the consequences are higher for those chosen to lead. It was a tough lesson for me to learn, but I realize it now, and feel obligated to pay the information forward.

Additionally, there were questions surrounding a mysterious new car that my mother had suddenly acquired. I wasn't getting paid to play basketball in high school, but companies seeking celebrity athletes begin building relationships with standout players at a young age, and I was likely going to be investigated if I were to remain in Wichita. Therefore, I don't say this to sound boastful, but it appeared that I had gotten a little too big for Wichita, and it was time to take the show on the road. The other driving factor was to prepare for college.

Hargrave was one of several military schools that we considered, along with basketball powerhouses Oakhill, which is also in Virginia, and Wershington Prep in Connecticut. Oakhill had produced countless professional basketball players. Meanwhile, Hargrave was more known for an impressive alumni of football players including champions of two separate Super Bowls, Torry Holt and Bernie Cozar. Nonetheless, this school seemed to provide the best combination of athletic opportunity and academic preparation, and to be honest, improving my ACT and SAT scores was just as important as dominating on the court.

I have made many mistakes in life, but like I stated earlier, I don't have many regrets. However, I do hate that I never brought Coach Allen a state championship before leaving Wichita East. He was a great coach and role model, and was certainly deserving, so I feel like I let him down. The East High team was loaded with top talent at every position. As the top player in the state and by most accounts, one of the top in the country, I was the catalyst of the team. Then there was LaVerne Smith (Verne), whose father is on record as one of the fastest players to ever play for the Pittsburg Steelers. The athletic genes of the father were certainly passed on to Verne who at 6'4" had the quickness of a running back, the speed of a wide receiver, and the dexterity and mobility to play fluidly at the one, two, and three positions.

With my dominance in the paint and mid-range prowess combined with Verne's ability to slash and make plays in traffic we were a combination that wreaked fear in the hearts of competitors. Additionally, there were three more players on the team who went on to receive division one sports scholarships, with Jamaicus Ricks fist making a pit stop at Independence Junior College where he starred in football and basketball, eventually claiming honors as the top Junior College basketball player in the Jayhawk East Conference. We also had Juston White, who started his career with the Wichita State Shockers, then went on to complete his eligibility at Winston-Salem State University. We were so loaded with talent that our fist three players coming off the bench would have been starters for just about any other team in the city.

I could go on explaining why our team was the most talented in the state, but sometimes talent isn't enough. Honestly, we may have been so talented that we got in our own way. Not sure what happened, but one thing is for certain – after dominating the entire game, we lost the state semi-fi als game and failed to advance to the state championship. I hate to this day that my last game as an East High Blue Ace ended on a sour note, but I rejoice at the winning legacy that I helped usher in at Hargrave.

As I stated before, prior to my arrival, Hargrave was known for football, but had yet to develop a winning reputation for basketball. In 1997, Oak Hill was ranked number one nationally as they had been many times previously. Wershington Prep was also nationally ranked in the top ten. Hargrave had never been ranked, but immediately jumped up to number five upon my signing. At point guard, we were fortunate to have Anthony Grundy, who went on to play for North Carolina State, and then for a brief spell with the Atlanta Hawks. Lavar Hemphill (the two-guard) had a successful career at Old Dominion University as well as overseas. Additionally, at power forward, we had Lonnie Baxter, Maryland NCAA Champion and NBA veteran. Since we had Lonnie at 6'9" in the post and Garvin Davis standing at 7' at center, this gave me the opportunity to play small forward. I had played center at Wichita East, so this enabled me to develop and showcase an array of skills that I was previously restricted from demonstrating.

Even at the small forward position, I led the team in scoring and rebounding. I was the fi st McDonalds All-American and fi st Parade All-American in the school's history. Since then, there have been three additional All-Americans. More importantly, there were no NBA players from Hargrave prior to my arrival. Largely due to my presence, the

Hargrave Tigers were able to attract future NBA superstars David West and Josh Howard the very next season. All-in-all, there have been 22 NBA players total who have come through Hargrave Academy since that time.

We fin shed the season with just one loss, to Wershington Prep. They were surprisingly amazing despite not having a single player who went on to play in the NBA. It was one of our fi st of a series of road games which included the junior varsity teams of several major colleges, junior college teams, and the West Point Military Academy Varsity team. As the season progressed, our team got better and better, and I would have loved to have played Wershington again later in the season. Nonetheless, I won't make any excuses – they were the best team the day they played us, and the reason we were not able to claim an undefeated season, fin shing with 33 wins and 1 loss.

For several years, basketball powerhouse Oakhill opened its season against Hargrave in what had become an annual grudge match. Previously, Hargrave had never defeated Oakhill, and they were just as loaded during my debut season as they had ever been, with future NBA star Corey Hightower, and other future NBA players Kevin Lyde, and Max Owens leading the roster. However, I refused to allow this to continue on my watch and on our home fl or. Oakhill would be coming to visit our gym, and this would be my opportunity to assert my presence on the prep basketball circuit.

Jerry Stackhouse and Rod Strickland were probably the biggest basketball names to grace the campus of Oakhill prior to my arrival at Hargrave. Since that time, they have continued to recruit the likes of Carmello Anthony, Kevin Durant, Rajon Rondo, and several others for a total of 34 NBA players, but history will always note that Korleone

Young was the first Hargrave leader to defeat this perennial basketball powerhouse. I finished the game with 33 points and 15 rebounds in a narrow three-point victory while leading Hargrave to its first ever victory over Oakhill.

Besides basketball, Hargrave provided me with the discipline needed to succeed at the next level (college or professional). Each day started early and typically ended at 9pm, with military formation at 6am. We would march to the cafeteria for breakfast which ended at 7:30, then we would break by table to prepare for class. Class was from 8am to noon, after which we would return to formation by 12:15 to prepare to march to lunch. Lunch typically ended at 1:15, and we had until 2pm to change into military attire and report for military time – a series of rigorous military drills and training. Military time ended at 4pm, and from 4pm to 5:30pm, there was basketball practice, then back in formation to march to dinner at 6:00pm. Immediately following dinner, there was study hall from 7pm to 8pm, then lastly there were two hours left to get ready for the next day, iron clothes, call home, and anything else that we needed to get done, then lights out by 10pm.

It was a strict and regimented environment, with severe punishment for disciplinary infractions. Not properly shining my boots, arriving late for the 6am formation, unsatisfactory room inspection, and missing curfew would result in pushups or marching for hours in a square area known as the bull ring. This was tough, but I wouldn't change it for the world. It was during this time that I met a gentleman named Sgt. Major Payne. During my time at Hargrave, Payne was the tactical officer. Today he is one of the top administrators of the school. For me, it was powerful to see someone on the campus who looked like me. In fact, Sgt. Major Payne was the only Black faculty member at Hargrave.

There is a movie titled "Major Payne" which stars Damon Wayans, and takes a comical approach to life at a prep school similar to Hargrave. It has been alleged that the hard-nosed and no-nonsense Payne portrayed by Wayans was derived from Hargrave's very own Sgt. Major Payne. I'm not certain whether or not this is true, but I am certain that there was great value in having a Black man on campus as a role model and disciplinarian. I think I can speak for all of the men who have come through Hargrave, and not just the Black men, when I say that Payne was an inspiration to us all.

Aunt Kathy and Cousin Deon

Military Formation

CHAPTER 8

•

AAU BASKETBALL

Pre-CMH 76ers

Prior to playing for the CMH (Children's Mercy Hospital) 76ers, my experience with summer basketball was as one would expect for a high school athlete - a few tournaments in neighboring states, and eight-to-ten local games against other high school athletes in the region. Other than playing with older kids, my pre-CMH experiences were fairly humble.

One of my first coaches was Tyrone Berry, with whom I am still friends with today. Coach Berry coached me on his sixth and seventh grade team while I was a fifth grader. By eighth grade, I moved on to play 17-and-under for the Wichita Jets, coached by former Wichita State Shockers player Gary Cundiff. All the other players on our team, as well as our competitors, were juniors and seniors in high school. Despite playing up and still dominating, I went unnoticed on the national scene until the Jets played a tournament in Long Beach, California. This tournament pushed me into the top five of all eighth graders throughout the country.

Along with my teammate DeAngelo Evans (former University of Nebraska running back), I made the all-tournament team. Ths was significant first because I was only 14 competing against 17-year-old seniors, and secondly because older players in attendance included the likes of Stephon Marbury, Paul Pierce, Tyron Liu, and countless other future pros. After watching me play, two players from CMH ap-proached me – Myron Piggie, Jr., and JaRon Rush. Coach John Walker called my mother asking my mother if I could join their team.

New Team – New Family

It started out with my taking US Air to Kansas City every weekend for practice. I left school at noon to catch a 1:30 flight. We practiced Fri-day and Saturday from 4-6pm. When in KC, I resided in the home of a wealthy booster for both the CMH 76ers and the Kansas Jayhawks. The house was unlike anything I had ever seen – an exquisite mansion with a sprawling estate, complete with swimming pool, sports court, and guest house.

After practice, my teammate (Myron Piggie) would leave with his father Myron Piggie Sr. Watching Piggie and his father interact remind-ed me of conversations with my grandfather. I was bored being in a big lonely mansion, and Piggie seemed as if he came from surroundings similar to mine. As my friendship with my teammates grew, I finally built up the nerve to ask if I could spend the night. This is when I really got to know Myron Sr., and would soon discover that we were blood relatives.

I was on the phone with my grandmother, and Piggie request-ed the phone to reassure my family that I was in good hands. As the conversation progressed, we discovered that my great-grandmother and his grandmother were sisters. Not only was I part of an elite team, but I was actually with family. I couldn't have been happier!

By the time I reached my sophomore year, I began spending summers traveling throughout the country, flying on private jets, residing in 4 and 5-star resorts, fi e dining, and various other perks. Playing for the CMH (Children's Mercy Hospital) 76ers was accompanied by a lifestyle that I had previously only dreamed of.

I remember neighborhood friends inquiring about games, wanting to come out and support me, and the look in their eyes when I would give them our game schedule. "Th s week we're in New Orleans, and next week Vegas, then Long Beach the following week." Most looked at me puzzled, and others asked "aren't you just fourteen or fi een?" Now that I'm older, I understand their disbelief. It wasn't realistic to believe that young athletes were living the life of rock stars, and traveling with NBA-worthy accommodations.

Major college programs, athletic apparel companies, and a group of individuals known as "handlers" lead the list of people who salivate over the idea of attaching themselves to a top-tier collegiate recruit or potential NBA prospect. As a result, we were treated like royalty wherever we traveled. While it is illegal for a high school player to be represented by an agent, the role of a handler, is essentially the same as that of an agent. If a college wants to contact a major recruit or his family, the communication is typically funneled through the handler even more so than the player's high school coach. My handler was also our summer coach, my cousin Myron Piggie, Sr. I've heard horror stories of handlers accepting money off the backs of kids or misleading kids, but from my perspective, this was never the case with Piggie. He truly looked out for our best interests, protected us, and always tried to negotiate the best possible scenario for each player on our team.

Myron Piggie, Sr.

Piggie's stout and muscular 5'9" physique and wide frame carry far more psychological weight than its physical 230 pounds. His thick short neck, shaved head, gold tooth, and menacing scowl, combined with facetious smirk, charming conversation, and streetwise smarts depict a character rivaling a mob figu e on one hand, and everyone's favorite uncle on the other. He always traveled with the team, and never met a stranger. Even people of celebrity status, including Michael Jordan, instantly fell in love with his boisterous laugh, brash personality, and unapologetic confide ce.

We were sponsored fairly well under Kansas Jayhawks boosters, but once we received additional sponsorship from a top sporting brand, everything changed. Mr. Walker stepped down, Piggie became our coach, and we immediately catapulted to the national spotlight. Soon after, Kansas City became a hub for premier AAU tournaments.

Piggie was as charming and charismatic as he was intimidating and hard-nosed. He leveraged these traits to negotiate a commitment from our sponsors that equated to hundreds of thousands of dollars in support for our team. Our wealthy boosters were very transparent of their intentions to convince our top players to become Kansas Jayhawks. These individuals arranged for Piggie a salary of nearly $50,000 to coach our team just for the summer. In addition to coaching CMH, Piggie was expected to deliver me and the Rush Brothers to the University of Kansas. Jaron and Kareem Rush were two of the top players in the country, and my teammates on the CMH summer team.

I'm not sure how serious any of us were about becoming Jayhawks to begin with. It wouldn't matter. Coach Williams instantly became less interested in Jaron when during an interview, he referred to Coach Williams as Roy, and publicly criticized the Kansas Jayhawk offense. Once Williams lost interest in Jaron, we all lost interest in becoming Kansas Jayhawks. With that, the team lost its sponsorship from wealthy Kansas alum, and its corporate endorsement. The team also lost its older players, which included me and Jaron. Under the new name, the KC Rebels, Piggie's team continued to dominate under the leadership of the younger Rush brother, Kareem. Kareem Rush spent his final AAU season dominating without the help of me and Jaron. He also went on to win one state title without his brother, with whom he had shared back-to-back titles the two prior seasons.

My Teammates

Kareem and Jaron Rush were both of Kansas City. Kareem had a great college career with the Missouri Tigers and was drafted in the first round of the 2002 NBA draft. Our primary guards included our coach's son, Myron Piggie, Jr, who had a solid college career with the UNLV (University of Nevada Las Vegas) Running Rebels; Corey Maggette who played one season for the Duke Blue Devils before being drafted in the first round of the 1999 NBA draft; and Earl Watson, who spent several years as both a player and a coach after playing for the UCLA Bruins and being drafted in the second round of the 2001 NBA draft.

Earl and Myron were both from Kansas City, but Corey was from Chicago. We had the financial means to go out and recruit whomever we wanted, so we reached out to Corey after seeing him dominate in summer league competition with another team. Similar can be said for our recruitment of Ryan Humphrey of Tulsa, Oklahoma. Ryan later became a fi st round pick in the 2002 draft after playing two years for the Oklahoma Sooners and two years for the Notre Dame Fighting Irish. Several other great players passed through our roster as well, including South Dakota resident and lottery pick in the 2000 NBA draft, Mike Miller. Our team was so loaded with talent that even with being a 6'8" sharp-shooter, Miller had trouble fi ding playing time and eventually left the team. Future NBA veteran Maurice Evans and several others passed through as well. From top to bottom, our team was loaded with future professionals, McDonald All-Americans, and high division one prospects at every position.

During our travels, we stumbled across a loaded Riverside Catholic Church team from New York. Meta World Peace (formally Ron Artest), Eric Barkley, Anthony Glover, Ricardo Greer, and Elton Brand all played for Riverside, who beat us pretty handily during our fi st encounter. Since they were a little older than we were, Piggie wasn't too upset the fi st time they defeated us. The second time, he was livid, but he had a right to be upset. With prospective professionals Corey Maggette, Earl Watson, Kareem Rush, Jaron Rush and myself, we were far too loaded with talent to continue being embarrassed by Riverside. To add insult to injury, we lost the second game on our home court, at our home tournament - the CMH Invitational.

The revenge game was more like a fist fi ht than a basketball game, with players going back and forth for one dazzling play after the next, with aggressive taunting to boot. Anthony Glover started it out with a massive dunk, then yelled out "we're gonna kill Kansas City." Following Glover's dunk, I dribbled the length of the court and across the baseline, before turning and dunking on their entire team, yelling profanity and disrespectful slurs towards the New York bench. I'm shocked that there were no technical fouls called, but the offi als allowed us to keep playing aggressively, physically, and with blatant disrespect for one another. Unfortunately, we lost to Riverside once again.

Jaron Rush Korleone Young Corey Maggette

The following season they came back to our tournament, this time without Artest and Brand, yet still just as talented. We would fi ally get our revenge in a 6-point win at Haskell College in Lawrence, Kansas. Other than Riverside, there weren't too many elite teams that we hadn't fared well against. However, after Piggie's continued emphasis, we realized that it was never a matter of talent. They were just mentally tougher than we were.

Investigation

With the influx of excessive exposure and tremendous talent, our team became a focal point of investigation and scrutiny. The overwhelming bulk of this controversy centered on Coach Piggie. It was alleged that Piggie had defrauded four universities – UCLA, Missouri, Duke, and Oklahoma State, paying just under $40,000 to five players, which declared them professionals and thus ineligible to compete as amateur collegiate players. I'm not sure whether these payments were truly made or not, but I do know that if such were the case, there were more people involved than just Piggie. However, our sponsors, wealthy boosters, and wealthy coaches, were all exempt from punishment, and the full burden fell on Piggie with ensuing consequences for Corey and Kareem, and more harsh consequences for me and Jaron.

Despite some reports claiming that Corey and Jaron left school to test NBA draft waters, the reality was that both were more or less pushed away due to these allegations. After averaging 11 points 7 rebounds and making the Pac-10 All Freshmen team his fi st season, Jaron was poised to dominate as a sophomore, but was suspended 24 games in 1999. Kareem was a freshman in 1999, and was suspended for 9 games during the same season. Despite the set-back, Kareem returned to claim co-freshmen of the year honors averaging 15ppg. Jaron returned for one game, hitting a buzzer beater to defeat top-ranked Stanford to advance to the sweet-16. Following tournament elimination, Rush declared for the NBA draft, but was undrafted despite many believing he would be a fi st round pick.

I hate that the world never got the opportunity to see the most electrifying small forward that I ever shared the court with. With the two of us being the premier players of the CMH team, the biggest spotlight fell on us once the Piggie investigation began. For Rush, this would mean going undrafted to the NBA. For me, it would result in my draft stock dropping drastically from being an early to middle fi st-round projection, to eventually being taken with the 40th pick. Piggie was eventually sentenced to prison. Jaron and I were punished for our association with Piggie.

Despite how any of this sounds, Piggie is not a bad guy. In fact, when it comes to protecting us, you couldn't fi d one better. The reality that most fail to realize is that nearly every elite player has a Piggie somewhere on their team, and with corporate sponsors, high profile collegiate programs, and NBA teams all taking notes, it's necessary to have someone around who can shield a kid and his family from the madness of all of this. Unfortunately, large corporations and prestigious institutions are far too revered to have their names caught up in business dealings that are often morally clouded. Therefore, the "Piggie's" of the world stand at the forefront accepting all the exposure, assuming all the risk, and taking it on the chin so that players like myself can hopefully achieve the dream of playing in the NBA. Meanwhile, new players are born daily. Like many others before and after us, Jaron and I were easy to dispose of.

The pipeline of future prospects is so abundant that it has become easy for top coaches, programs, and apparel brands to lose interest in one player and move on to the next rising star. Th s system is unforgiving and cares very little about past performance or accolades. It is instead an environment that rewards and punishes in real time. Players who were at one moment idolized, become barbershop whispers of what could've, should've, and would've happened in the very next moment. Some kids make it out of this vicious cycle and obtain enormous opportunity and wealth. Others become fall guys for a system that is only concerned about bottom line dollars, winning programs, and selling shoes, but could care less about the kids it exploits.

Though teenagers, AAU basketball quickly forced us to become men. Sure, we had the age and maturity of kids, but were instead essentially products for exchange in a big business cycle. Top-tier youth sports programs represent money, strong corporate presence, and involvement from highly influential people, but it doesn't represent child's play. For something as simple as kids running up and down a wooden fl or, attempting to place a round ball into a round hole, the energy surrounding the game is one of high stakes. With any high stake business, there are consequences when things don't transpire as expected. Beneath the flashing lights and glamour of the NBA are talented and often impoverished Black kids who are treated as commodities rather than human beings. Some weather the storm and reach massive wealth and superstardom, while others falter and become unknown.

Myron Piggie

I can accept failure, everyone fails at something. But I can't accept not trying.

I've failed over and over and over again in my life and that is why I succeed.

Michael Jordan

CHAPTER 9

•

Michael Jordan Flight School

The Michael Jordan Basketball Camp is branded the Michael Jordan Flight School. The camp started in 1995, so it was just in its third year when I attended in 1997. I had the luxury of attending all the best camps in the nation, but this was by far the best experience. Not only were campers exposed to the best training imaginable, we also had the opportunity to compete with the man who most consider the greatest player of all times, Michael Jordan.

The scheduled camp day started each morning at 8:00 am and ended at roughly 9:30 at night, unlike most camps which conclude between 5pm and 6pm. Once younger campers were asleep, Jordan would host some of the most grueling late night pick-up games I've ever experienced. In fact, Jordan's legendary pick-up games were probably more intense than AAU and prep school competition combined.

Elite college players served as camp counselors during the day, but during late night games, top high school talent and college stars participated in intense bouts that ended near midnight. Many of the nation's top college players attend each year. The 1997 camp took place just months after the Arizona Wildcats defeated Jordan's Alma matter – the North Carolina Tar Hills in the NCAA fi al four. Arizona went on to defeat the Kentucky Wildcats and claim the 1997 NCAA championship. They had earlier defeated number one ranked Kansas in the sweet 16 on the road to a complete sweep of three of the four schools that arguably house the nation's most storied college basketball programs - programs commonly known as the blue bloods (Kansas, North Carolina, Kentucky, and UCLA).

The recent documentary "The Last Dance" depicts Jordan as a fi rce competitor who holds grudges as means of feeding his insatiable competitive edge. I witnessed this fi st hand as he intentionally punished, intimidated, and verbally abused players from both teams (North Carolina and Arizona). He made it obvious that he was upset with North Carolina players for losing, and Arizona players for defeating, his precious alma mater.

Arizona was led by its dynamic backcourt of Miles Simon and Mike Bibby. Simon was the tournament's highest scorer and also received the award for the tournament's Most Outstanding Player (MOP). Bibby went on the following draft year to become an NBA lot-tery pick as the second overall player taken in the 1998 draft. Though finishing just third in conference play at 11-5, the North Carolina Tar Hills had two future NBA superstars in Antawn Jamison and Vince Carter who were taken fourth and fifth respectively in the 1998 draft. With the size and strength of Jamison and the athleticism of Carter, the Tar Hills were ripe for NCAA tournament success. However, de-spite these virtually unstoppable players, North Carolina was incapa-ble of advancing past Arizona, and Jordan was outright mad about it, as we all would discover.

Jordan insisted that the high school players play on his team, which put me and my AAU teammates Jaron Rush and Earl Watson with him. Simon, Bibby, Jamison, and Carter played together on the opposing team. At 17 years of age, I was star struck by not only Jordan, but also with these college stars whose celebrity rivaled that of many professionals.

Based on how competitive he was as a pick-up game teammate, I can't begin to imagine how intense he must have been as an NBA teammate, especially during playoffs and fi als. Jordan's grudge about the North Carolina loss to Arizona would result in all responsible parties of both teams, soon having hell to pay. Games only went to twelve points, but were as intense as a double overtime regulation game. Of course, if Jordan's team was losing by the time 12 points were reached (which was rare), games could go up to as high as 30 points. His camp, his rules!

Jordan was so competitive and intense that he was outright mean as he continually transitioned his game to exploit these young college stars, dominating each of them in their own respective areas of strength. Carter was known for his athleticism and monster dunks, and Jamison for his strength and power in the post. Jordan would alter between bullying Jamison in the post and playing above the rim in a manner that Carter could only envy, but not emulate. Every turnaround jump shot, picturesque dunk, and eloquent drive to the basket was accompanied by obscenities of how worthless they were as players and human beings for losing to Arizona. He was outraged that Jamison and Carter had let North Carolina down, and was intent on punishing them for such.

Bibby and Simon were known for quickness, speed, and ball handling prowess, so he embarrassed the two of them with breathtaking perimeter moves and open court mastery, yelling out similar obscenities, expressing that there is no way they would have beaten North Carolina on his watch, then calling Jamison and Carter everything from bums to far worse for allowing such to happen under their regime. The only way to stop the trash talk and intimidating gestures was to beat Jordan, which no one was able to do. Meanwhile, he continued to punish these college kids with each dribble, each shot, and each harsh word that escaped his lips.

I watched in awe as I did my best to balance between being amazed, with being a competitive teammate. Meanwhile, he effortlessly dominated the top college players in the nation with the ease of an adult defeating a small child in a foot race. It was just as artistic as it was brutal, and as poetic as it was barbaric. Jordan's desire is not just to win, but to embarrass, intimidate, and destroy his competition, and he made good on each of these desires.

I believe the children are our future, teach them well and let them lead the way. Show them all the beauty they possess inside. Give them a sense of pride to make it easier. Let the children's laughter remind us how we used to be...

George Benson lyrics made famous by Whitney Houston

CHAPTER 10

•

Mere Child's Play

I have enjoyed the good fortune of experiencing basketball as both an observer and an active participant. Despite my lengthy involvement with the sport, its dynamic nature never ceases to amaze me. However, if you strip the game to its most primitive, simplistic, and organic form, basketball is similar to kickball, tag, hide-and-seek, or any other game that children play. Take away the thousands of fans in attendance and the millions watching on television, and what do you really have? Once you remove the lucrative endorsement deals and the fancy athletic apparel, or the bright lights, fancy cars, and pretty girls, what you truly have is grown men engaged in a game that kids play. Highly skilled, extremely competitive, and executed and performed by some of the world's most elite athletic specimen, yet a game nonetheless. In his book "Sweet Sweet Blues on the Road," Wynton Marsalis refers to his life as a jazz musician as "grown men engaged in mere child's play." In a sense, I guess I look at basketball in the same manner.

Once the multiple, complex, and fascinating layers of glamour and celebrity fanfare are unraveled, the bright lights of massive arenas named for major corporations are not much different from the city lights that illuminate asphalt covered playgrounds in project housing courtyards. Inner city playgrounds throughout the country are the types of places where impoverished boys began their journey toward becoming some of basketball's greatest legends. But the game of basketball is even simpler than that when we continue to peel back layers and move closer to its core.

At its purest form, the game of basketball is the culmination of a harsh New England winter in December 1891 and the rowdy nature of young boys who couldn't play outside… At its purest form, basketball is a Springfield Massachusetts YMCA, where a thirty-year-old employee named Naismith became frustrated with a restless group of adolescent male members of the YMCA where he was employed, and was tasked with creating an indoor game that would provide an athletic distraction to calm the boys down while keeping them in shape for track season… At its purest form, basketball is nothing more than the two peach baskets that Naismith nailed to each end of the YMCA gymnasium, a soccer ball, the 18 young men who engaged in its inaugural 9-on-9 game, and the posting of 13 rules on the wall…

The original copy of basketball's 13 rules were purchased at auction by University of Kansas alum David Booth for $4.3 million dollars in 2010, whereas at the very same auction, a copy of the emancipation proclamation signed by Abraham Lincoln sold for just $3.7 million. Examples like this make it easy to forget the pure and simple nature of the game, but even this record-breaking auction in many ways symbolizes the simplicity of basketball.

How on earth could a game that demands such a massive auction price fail to supersede the humility that sits at the core of the sport?

When we think about things like humility, family values, hard work, and a common existence, the state of Kansas is arguably the state that comes to mind. Th s sentiment is even depicted in the classic film "The Wizard of Oz." The main character is Dorothy, a simple girl who desires nothing more than to return to her simple home and simple life in Kansas. After following a road of yellow bricks on a fascinating journey across magical and mystical terrain, Dorothy remains steadfast in asserting that "there is no place like home." Therefore it is only fitting that after an incredible 119 year journey that the foundation rules of basketball were returned to their rightful home – the same place that Dorothy called home – the same place that David Booth calls home – and the same place that I call home – Kansas, the cradle for the sport of basketball.

If you are unaware, you may be asking - why do the 13 original rules belong in Kansas if they were created in Massachusetts? True students of the game understand the connection between the great state of Kansas and the beautiful game of basketball, but the uninitiated may be unaware, so I will explain. Just seven years after its creation, the game's inventor, Dr. James Naismith (an actual medical doctor) arrived at the University of Kansas in 1898 as the school's fi st basketball coach. Though he is the only coach in the history of the school with a losing record (55 wins and 60 losses) he came in contact with a young player named Forrest "Phog" Allen, who became the second coach of the University of Kansas Jayhawks. Under the direction of Allen emerged two native Kansans who went on to develop two of the most storied programs in the sport. Adolph Rupp, from Halstead, Kansas, played for Allen from 1920 to 1923 and was a member of Allen's back-to-back national championship teams (Helms Championships which preceded the current NCAA championship model). Dean Smith, from Halstead, Kansas, played for Allen's 1952 NCAA championship team.

As history informs us, these two men went on to develop two of the winningest and most envied programs in the history of college basketball – Smith with the North Carolina Tar Hills and Rupp with the Kentucky Wildcats. Even with Rupp being removed from coaching since 1972 and Smith since 1997, their respective wins of 879 in 36 seasons, and 876 in 41 seasons still stand as number five and six on the all-time winningest coaches list. However, the influence of these two Kansas natives goes far beyond their achievements as both coaches and players. While it is noteworthy to mention the likes of legendary coach Pat Riley and perhaps the game's most storied player Michael Jordan playing for Coach Rupp and Coach Smith respectively, even these names and countless other legends fail to measure the impact that the state of Kansas has had on the global phenomenon known as basketball.

My opinion is that social justice is far more important than wins and losses, storied careers, and legendary names. Therefore, it is signifi ant to note the role that both Smith and Rupp played in the game becoming desegregated. What I am about to say is in no way a slap in the face to the legacy of coach Rupp, and both stories are important, but the role of these two legends is as different as night and day with regards to social justice. Th ough the lens of equality as it pertains to basketball, Smith asserted himself as a champion for racial equality when he used his influence to recruit the Tar Hill's fi st African American scholarship athlete, Charlie Scott in 1967. Smith was also adamant in advocating that local North Carolina businesses treat African Americans fairly and equally.

While Rupp was indeed a great coach and truly one of the game's greatest pillars, his social justice story is one in which he is not the hero. Rupp, who was alleged as saying that he would never have a Black player on the University of Kentucky team would find himself coaching in what was arguably the most racially charged championship game that college basketball has ever witnessed – the 1966 NCAA Championship game between the Kentucky Wildcats and the Texas Western Miners (now the University of Texas at El Paso or UTEP). The game marked the first time in history that an all-black starting five took the court against an all-white team in a national championship game.

Whether or not Rupp was a racist is a question that continues to be debated, but is not the important theme. What is more significant is the manner in which this one game changed the landscape of college sports forever. Many consider it the most important sporting event ever to be played, while others have gone as far as calling it the Brown vs. Board of Education (Brown v. BOE) of college sports. Since the 1954 Brown v. BOE case took place in Kansas as well, it is poetic justice for college sports desegregation to also have Kansas ties. The game that was played less than one year after the signing of the Voting Rights Act of 1965, ended with the heavily favored and all-white Kentucky Wildcats being convincingly defeated by the Texas Western Miners in a sporting event that was instrumental in integrating college sports throughout the country.

For me, the story is even more touching and personal because of the role that it plays in cementing my home state as a significant fixture in the history of basketball. There are less than six degrees of separation between the state of Kansas and some of history's finest coaches, its most celebrated legends, and its role in advancing social justice and racial equality. As the 10th player in history ever drafted to the NBA directly out of high school, I feel privileged to have my name included as part of this rich Kansas basketball history.

So herein lies the question that brings us back to where we started - why on earth would the demand be so great to watch the best athletes in the world play a game designed for kids? Even noble public servants who educate our children and heroic individuals who run into burning buildings to save lives fail to garner the attention of scantily clad men attempting to place a ball into a hole. On paper it sounds silly, but anyone who has ever watched a game or played a game knows that the game of basketball is far too magical to be explained in logical and sensible language. Instead, it is best described by the boisterous screams of business men and women who yell at their television sets at the top of their lungs; barbershop conversations comparing Jordan to Kobe and LeBron; countless social media debates on a plethora of basketball-related subject matter; and the one time each year where the job responsibilities of millions are compromised by desires to become professional bracketologists.

Despite the fact that its enthusiasm is beyond explanation, the late Kobe Bryant may have captured it best in his love letter to the game entitled "Dear Basketball". In the five-minute animated film, Bryant explains through basketball, the imagination of every young boy to become great at something. Bryant's journey from a child shooting socks into make- believe baskets to becoming a five-time world champion provides inspiration that is of greater signifi ance than what can be encompassed by the game itself. Instead, it is a compelling challenge for kids to dream, aspire, and work towards becoming excellent. It is an inspiring challenge supporting the notion that we all have the power to change the world. Whether a kid wants to become a professional athlete, a fi efi hter, a school teacher, or anything else, Kobe's letter to basketball reminds us all that everything that we aspire to become begins with a dream to become the very best possible version of ourselves.

So the popularity of the game that I have always loved can be summed up as a reminder to adults of a time when we were dreamers. It reinforces the excuse to tap into innocent and childish energies that accompany not having a care in the world. The song lyrics of "The Greatest Love of All" by George Benson, later recorded by Whitney Houston strengthen this notion, stating "Let the children's laughter, remind us how we used to be." In a sense, we all miss the freedom and adventure that coincides with our youth, and basketball gives us an excuse to escape adulthood for brief moments, and vicariously relive our childhood through the exploits of some of the world's most gifted athletes. Basketball is arguably one of the only mechanisms in society where folks from all walks of life share the commonality of escaping reality together to cheer, boo, laugh, hiss, converse, debate, celebrate, and dream together! In a sense, one could say that basketball and diversity are one in the same.

Like Kobe, and I imagine like most everyone else, I too love to dream. Similar to Kobe, my dream was to play in the NBA. I imagine that there is a physician or a police office somewhere who played doctor or cop with the same passion that I did in pretending to be a professional athlete, so I truly believe the dream to be the seed to any child's growth regardless of their aspirations. My childhood fantasy was to one day play for the Detroit Pistons. My favorite player had always been Magic Johnson, but my favorite team was without question, the Pistons.

Let me remind you again that I come from Kansas, where airplane manufacturing is the dominant industry, which in some ways shares similarities with Detroit, where motor vehicles are mass produced. The Pistons always seemed to have a blue collar image that matched the mentality of the city. They were a group of hardnosed, hardworking, and no nonsense guys who were so tough, they were branded the "Bad Boys" through the late 80s and early 90s. Branded so well in fact, that even Nelson Mandela was photographed in a Pistons jacket and hat.

While the NBA experienced massive and well-needed rebranding under the glamourous rivalry of Larry Bird and Magic Johnson, Pistons players such as Vinny Johnson, Rick Mahorn, and Dennis Rodman didn't necessarily have the boyish good looks and magnetic charisma of Magic Johnson. Meanwhile, the affluent upbringing of Bill Laimbeer failed to touch heart strings like the Cinderella story of Bird – the poor white kid from French Lick, Indiana. Though the charming smile and fie ce competitive nature of Isiah Thomas was Hollywood worthy, his persona was certainly no match for the backstory of two throwback white guys (Larry Bird and Kevin McHale) existing as one of the greatest forward tandems in the history of the game, or the fast paced excitement of Magic, Kareem, Worthy and the Showtime Lakers. Even players like Mark Aguirre, Joe Dumars, and John Salley were amazing athletes with impressive resumes, but playing in Detroit does not garner the same attention as playing for the Celtics, perhaps the most storied franchise in the history of the sport, or the Lakers, where home games resemble a who's who celebrity guest list that rivals the Academy Awards. Therefore, no one would argue that the Pistons were not the most glamourous team in the league. However, very few would argue that they were not the toughest.

With the mentality of factory workers and the precision of assembly line manufacturing, the Pistons played the game in a manner that mirrored the day-to-day grind of working class America. I was 10 and 11-years old during their 1989 and 1990 back-to-back championship seasons, during which time both my mother and my Aunt Cathy worked on airplane assembly lines. I guess rooting for the Pistons seemed like rooting for my mother and aunt, and seeing the Pistons win was like seeing a win for my mother, my Aunt Cathy, and all of those around me who work hard and grind daily. In a sense, seeing the Pistons win was like seeing my hometown win!

To fully understand what is special about the Detroit Pistons requires understanding the former home of the team, the Palace of Auburn Hills. By defin tion, a palace is a royal residence. Therefore, it was appropriate that an arena of such a name be built in the city that became home to sports royalty the likes of Joe Lewis, Gordy Howe, Ty Cobb, and eventually Barry Sanders. I wanted so badly to become a part of this culture, and to my disbelief, this dream would come true. From a nostalgic standpoint, it couldn't have come at a better time. Joe Dumars was the last member of the Bad Boys team still actively playing during my rookie season, and the entire Bad Boys roster would be coming to celebrate the 10-year reunion as this would likely be the fi al season for Dumars. While it didn't turn out as I had imagined in my mind, this was symbolic of the palace guards ushering out the Bad Boys legends while ushering me in to take the reign as part of the new Pistons legacy. Despite this never happening, I was part of the Pistons' team for this historic event. Th s is a memory that I will cherish forever.

The game was played on April 3, 1999 and featured the marquee match-up between two of the games emerging superstars, Penny

Hardaway and Grant Hill. Hill fin shed the game with an impressive 19 points on 7 of 14 shooting, but was no match for Penny's 30 points on nearly 65% from the fi ld. Despite a crushing 92-77 loss for the Pistons, being in the presence of so many legends was breathtaking. What was even more surreal was that Dominique Wilkins was one of my favorite players as a small child, and he too was participating as a member of the Orlando Magic. When Wilkins began his career in 1982, I was just three years old, and now here we were, two grown men, engaged in child's play together, both playing professional basketball in the NBA.

Wow, dreams really do come true! My hope is that through my story, others can be inspired to know that their dreams can become a reality as well, regardless of what those dreams may be. I want my story to also serve as a lesson that informs others that in the same breath that a wish is granted, it can also be taken away. Th s is why I work so hard at encouraging kids to never stop working and never becoming complacent. Lastly, I want my story to serve as one of resilience. I would have loved to have retired with millions of dollars after a legendary career, but it didn't happen. However, giving up was never an option then and it isn't an option now. My message to you is that while life may knock you down, it's up to you not to allow it to knock you out. Get up, keep fi hting, and keep reaching for your goals and I promise, you will not lose. The only real losses we encounter in this life take place when we give up and quit on ourselves.

Identity is a prison you can never escape, but the way to redeem your past is not to run from it, but to try to understand it, and use it as a foundation to grow...

Jay Z (Shawn Carter)

CHAPTER 11

•

The Tale of Two Draft Nights

Charles Dickens described the French Revolution as both "the best of times and the worst of times" in the classic novel "A Tale of Two Cities." For me, the 2016 draft night represented a similar bitter-sweet discourse. The date was June 23, 2016, and I was as eager to watch the draft as I had ever been. The NBA draft has been a special event for me as far back as I can recall. As a kid I would sit in front of the television in amazement as names were called to join the elite fraternity comprised of the best basketball players in the world. I remember hometown legends Darnell Valentine and Antoine Carr being drafted to the league, and my dream was fueled by knowing that players from right here in my home town had become some of the world's elite players. Many days I would consume myself with dreams of my name being called, until one day in 1998 it really happened.

I am a living witness that dreams do come true and that hard work does pay off. When I speak to kids in public settings or even just in passing, one of the main points I try to get across is not to be afraid to dream and to dream big. Additionally, it is equally important not to be afraid to put forth the work that it will take to make dreams become reality. Th s is a philosophy that applies to every facet of life and not just sports. Even now, I am revamping the same philosophies of dreaming and hard work that got me to the NBA and applying them towards my new dream of building a business designed to help others with goal setting, physical fitness, and developing the mentality to see their dreams through to fruition.

Other than my own draft night in 1998, I had never anticipated a draft in the manner that I had the 2016 draft. Another standout Wichita athlete was expecting to be inducted into the exclusive brotherhood that I was once fortunate to be a part of, and I was elated that he would be getting this opportunity. In my own selfish way, I guess I looked at it as having a chance to relive the excitement of my own draft. I've been following Perry Ellis since he was in middle school and was always impressed with him on and off the court. In some ways, the two of us are similar.

Like me, Perry too was a McDonald's All-American in high school and one of the top college recruits in the nation. Although our paths of getting to draft night were as opposite as night and day, we were similar from the standpoint that we were both from Wichita, Kansas and both of us found ourselves waiting eagerly to hear our name called on NBA draft night. Though my own draft took place 18 years prior, I found myself watching Perry's draft with the same nervous energy that I experienced when I was in his position, watching pick after pick expire, hoping to hear his name called just as I had waited nervously to hear my own name nearly two decades earlier.

Based on Wichita being a somewhat small city, one would think the two of us had some sort of relationship. We barely know each other outside of both being the subject of local barbershop sports conversations. Nonetheless, I had become a big fan and had cheered for him with the same excitement as if we had been the best of friends. As I watched the draft, I sat on the edge of my seat waiting to erupt in joy once Perry's name was called. On June 23, 2016, NBA Commissioner Adam Silver walked up to the podium to begin the draft, but in my mind, I could see previous commissioner David Stern as my thoughts kept reverting back to June 24, 1998. Silver calmly blurted out the following words, "With the fi st overall pick of the 2016 NBA Draft, the Philadelphia Seventy-Sixers select Ben Simmons of Louisiana State University," but in my mind, I was 18 years old again, feeling the same nervousness as I did hearing Michael Olowokandi's name being called by Mr. Stern to start the 1998 draft.

The anxiety that I felt in 1998 continued with each pick as I continued to wait for Ellis's name to be announced. "With the sixth overall pick, the Sacramento Kings select Buddy Hield!" Hield played some of his high school ball for a prep school in Wichita and had played on the same AAU team with Ellis, so I got excited with a pick that felt close to home. "Certainly, he will be drafted now" I said to myself, thinking back to the sixth pick of my draft class, the late Robert Traylor. Traylor and I had become pretty good friends during rookie transition camp, and I assumed that Ellis and Hield had a decent relationship, so in my own warped way of connecting the dots, I convinced myself that this was some type of sign that Ellis would be drafted.

Th oughout the evening, several other names were announced, but Perry seemed to continue being passed over. I reminisced back to

1998 once again, sitting nervously in a crowded bar occupied by family, friends, and spectators wondering if it was ever going to happen. I remember thinking to myself how embarrassing it would be to go undrafted while in the company of so many supporters. I wondered whether Ellis was in similar surroundings, how he was feeling, and what his thoughts were. Here I was in my late 30's, but reliving every second of a critical moment of my teenage life through the life of a stranger for the most part.

Though I would reap none of the rewards, hearing Ellis's name would be like hearing mine all over again. I thought to myself, "certainly this kid will be drafted – he did everything right!" Meanwhile, my mind drifted to my own thoughts during this time in my life. I had exceptional workouts and interviewed well but waited and wondered as my chances lessened with every pick. I thought back to prominent coaches and general managers stating with confide ce, "We're taking him", after my workouts, then having the life sucked out of me as each of them passed me up for other talented players. I could not help but wonder how many broken promises may have been made to Ellis in the same manner.

There is such an argument made claiming a need for prep athletes to attend college, and here is a kid that not only attended college but graduated with honors. Commissioner Silver continued calling names, and I specifi ally remember the names of 25th and 32nd picks. These two picks were significant in my draft in 1998, since two of my competitive rivals were taken with these picks. "With the 25th pick, the Indiana Pacers select, Al Harrington of St. Patrick's High School" and "with the 32nd pick, the Seattle Supersonics select Rashad Lewis" is what may as well had said when the names of Brice Johnson and Ivica Zubac were announced.

I had defeated both Harrington and Lewis in head-to-head competition and was never given the opportunity to prove that I was a better selection. Now I was hoping to live vicariously through Ellis who I was confide t could prove the same point, and I would eagerly await him to dominate Johnson and Zubac in competition to claim victory for himself, and unknowingly for me as well. It came to the 40th pick which is where I was drafted, and I convinced myself that Ellis would be drafted in this same position. As beautiful and poetic as that would have been for two hometown kids to be drafted at the same position, it did not happen. I continued to await the calling of his name, but it was never called and to my surprise, Ellis went undrafted.

My name has been used in almost every argument favoring athletes attending school before becoming NBA eligible, and here is a kid who is a strong proponent for education, a model citizen, and a flat out stellar player, and not a single NBA team found him worthy of a draft pick. Often, I wonder what direction my career would have taken had I attended school, and sometimes I even wonder whether various negative opinions about me are accurate. "Would my career have been more fruitful had I done two or three years in college?" I often think to myself as I hear the voices of others making such claims, but those same voices can be heard saying just the opposite about Ellis. "He would have been drafted had he come out early!" is a common sentiment shared regarding this dominant player and proven winner going undrafted.

There was a time that these contradicting thoughts would upset me, but with age and maturity, I no longer get mad about confli ting narratives. It is humorous to a certain degree if you think about it. After spending the past 18 years being told that not going to school cost me a lengthy NBA career, Ellis is being told that staying in school too long has cost him the same. The reality is that there is no science to this, and perhaps there is some truth in both arguments. Ironically, it seems that every sports fan in America believes that they have all the right answers. I guess it wouldn't be a multibillion dollar industry if people didn't think about it, talk about it, and convince themselves that they were experts!

There is a strange irony in the fact that the top NBA draft selections are called lottery picks. Just as playing the lottery consists of one hoping to blindly guess a set of random numbers for the chance of becoming wealthy, NBA hopefuls rely on some degree of luck in hopes of changing the life trajectory for themselves and their families. Unlike the cash lottery, NBA prospects have put in countless hours of work in preparing for draft night. However, with only 60 picks in the draft, there will always be players who are drafted and given spots over players who are just as, and in some cases, more talented than those selected. Many variables must be considered including, the right person seeing you play at the right time, coming from a certain AAU team, the political clout of your college coach or program, individual workouts, and various other factors. From the outside looking in, a good college season or a great March Madness performance seem to be deal solidifie s, and in some instances, they are; but the business of professional basketball is far too complex to categorize with one correct answer. Every player is different, every draft is different, and every single situation is different, with different answers, solutions, and outcomes.

Take another standout Wichita athlete for example. Adrian Griffi is a few years older than I am, but we share the same high school alma mater, Wichita High School East. Griffi eventually enjoyed a tenured

NBA career and still serves as a top assistant coach and world champion, so the game has treated him well. However, Griffin's road to the NBA was not an easy one. After finshing his senior season at Seaton Hall averaging 16 points and 8 rebounds per game, and making the All-Big East second team, Griffi was undrafted in the 1996 NBA draft. If ever there were a testimony of faith and hard work, Griffi would certainly fit the bill. Why he was undrafted is still a mystery to me, but instead of complaining, he worked tirelessly towards achieving his dream. He spent four years in college and another four years dominating professional leagues far less glamorous than the NBA. In fact, I imagine some of his games were less glamorous than major Big East games or even winning a Kansas State High School championship for that matter. Nonetheless, Griffi worked through the trenches without complaining, and found himself in a favorable position. I hope and pray that the same happens for Perry Ellis! I believe in my heart that it will.

CHAPTER 12

•

NBA: The Rookie

Welcome to the NBA

The league is slightly different now than it was in 1998. While we did have supports in place to assist rookies in becoming successful, it was nothing like the robust rookie orientation program that exists today. Instead, there was an expectation for tenured superstars to take young players under their wings and show them the ropes, along with the expectation that new players arrive with the mental, physical, and professional readiness for an NBA career. Ultimately, the NBA is a high exposure business with large revenues, and high stakes, so young players are expected to come into the league prepared, or be replaced by someone else. The enormous pressure of getting acclimated to playing at the NBA level is heightened by other factors, including being targeted by promiscuous women, shady business propositions, friends needing financial assistance, properly budgeting finances, and taking proactive measures to remain safe and protected.

My plan was quite simple – I would learn as much as I could from the staff and from my teammates. I was a huge fan of both Grant Hill and Christian Laettner. They were the star players for the back-to-back Duke championships in 1991 and 1992. I was also a fan of previously mentioned Charles O'Bannon who had won a college championship for the UCLA Bruins, alongside his brother Ed O'Bannon in 1995. I was excited to know that these three stellar players would soon become my teammates. I never attended college, so I assumed that the championship pedigree that each of them brought from their college days would be a great learning experience for my rookie season. Plus, Grant was rapidly emerging as one of the league's premier superstars and best players, so competing with him each day in practice would likely speed up my development process. The added bonus was that Joe Dumars was still playing, and so to go from growing up watching him play for my favorite team, to sharing the court with him would be a dream come true.

Of course, some things in life don't work out exactly as we envision them. For me, both the rookie transition period and the mentoring opportunities were cut short due to the 1998-1999 NBA lockout. I was drafted on June 24, 1998, but the lockout began on July 1 of the same year. It lasted until January 20, 1999. By the time the season started on February 5, 1999, we barely had two weeks to prepare.

For all practical purposes, I was in great physical shape, but not necessarily the type of conditioning that prepares a young player for the NBA. Sure, I had been running, lifting weights, and eating properly, but that only covers 80% of the mental and physical requirements needed to successfully compete with the world's elite athletes. The fi al 20% comes from the day-to-day grind in a world that includes elite players and trainers, seasoned coaches, and world class training facilities. Former Wichita State University guard and current NBA world champion Fred VanVleet summed it up nicely during an interview for a sports radio show. The host of the show made a comment about players needing to attend college for more development, to which Fred replied that despite loving every moment of his four years playing for the Wichita State Shockers, his fi st year of NBA development by far outweighed his four years of development in a college system. Th s was in no way a slight to Wichita State. He was simply expressing the reality that balancing basketball and school is no comparison to being a full-time professional athlete, with unlimited access to the best developmental environment imaginable.

Despite my reality being a far cry from my imagined transition of developing friendships with star players and learning the game from individuals I had previously idolized, I began to develop quickly, and became a dominant force in every practice. Far removed from the packed out games in Wichita, Kansas or the celebrity fanfare of the AAU circuit, I was now one of many young players whom the league felt made the transition to the NBA too soon. In fact, NBA Commissioner David Stern called me personally to suggest that I attend college rather than enter the draft. I found myself watching games from the bench, hoping, wishing, and praying for a chance to prove everyone wrong. Still a teenager, too young to buy a glass a beer or to gamble in the Windsor, Canada casinos that neighbor Detroit, I was left to fend for myself, prove that I belonged, and hopefully, once again become a recognizable name. I craved the opportunity to show the world what my teammates were already well aware of, but my coach never gave me the opportunity to shine.

Young Fella

I've always been slow to adjust to new surroundings, new experiences, and new friends. Th s was the case on both my fi st day of high school at Wichita East and my fi st day of military school at Hargrave. Arriving in Detroit for my rookie season with the Pistons required once again revisiting the nervous anxiety that accompanies entering new physical spaces and meeting new people. Th s time the fear was far more intense. I was 18-years-old, and not even a full year removed from high school. In a matter of months, I had gone from competing with 16 and 17-year-old kids, to facing the best basketball players in the world. Other than attending military academy, I had never been away from my mother and grandparents for any extended time period. Suddenly, I was alone and terrifi d in a new city, beginning a new career, all while learning to become an adult.

Miles away from the supports I had grown accustomed to, and extremely nervous, my life had suddenly become consumed with uneasiness and depression. As fie ce as I was known for being on the court, I was equally docile when consumed by emotion and fear. I even called home to my mother crying on several occasions. As embarrassing as this sounds coming from a grown man, my mother eventually came to Detroit to take care of me during a portion of training camp. Despite these and other emotional and psychological disconnects, I was eager to accept the challenge of becoming a pro, and joining my favorite team – The Detroit Pistons. I don't think I'm much different from anyone else. From kids attending a new school to adults beginning new careers, most of us approach new encounters with a certain degree of fear and insecurity. It's human nature for the most part. We work through the discomfort until eventually fi ding a place of comfort in our new surroundings, which I was eventually able to do with the Pistons.

Initially, I wasn't greeted with the warm welcome that I had expected. When arriving at Hargrave, I was embraced with celebrity fanfare. However, with the Pistons, I didn't even know the time and date of our fi st practice, and was too embarrassed to reach out to teammates to fi d out. We didn't receive a welcome packet or a printed schedule. At Hargrave and at Wichita East, we were pretty much told where to be, when to be there, and what to do once we arrived. Such nurturing and coddling ceases in the professional world. Instead, there is an expectation for players to be responsible, accountable, and proactive in meeting the rigorous obligations of professional basketball. I figu ed it out on my own, and walked into the fi st practice so nervous that my stomach felt as if it were sitting on top of my chest. From the coaches and trainers, to other players on the team, all eyes were on me as I entered the facility, as everything seemed to be moving in slow motion.

Immediately, veteran teammates began referencing me as "Young Fella." Th s name became my calling card throughout the shortened 50-game season. To be honest, I wouldn't be surprised if some of my teammates were unaware of what my name was. So "Young Fella" I became, and I would soon fi d out that the fi st day of practice would prove to be just as much about initiating me into the league as it was about learning the offense. Prior to training camp, I was incorrect in assuming that it wouldn't be much different from my existing workout regime. I had always worked out and taken care of my body, so I thought to myself that this shouldn't be too much more intense than other physical challenges previously faced.

Indeed I was in for a rude awakening! NBA training camp was the most physically exhausting, mentally challenging, full contact environment that one could imagine. Elite athletes, with abnormal size and strength, colliding into one another at heights three and four feet above the rim, diving for loose balls, and running at full speed defi es only a portion of camp. Out of respect for the veterans that serve our country, I don't want to compare it to war, but seeing blood and chipped teeth was a common occurrence. Superstars like Grant Hill and Jerry Stackhouse had guaranteed jobs, but many of us were still trying to prove that we belonged there. The competition was fie ce and typically not friendly. We all knew that making the roster would potentially empower us to provide for our families, so earning a position was like winning the lottery. With several players competing for a fin te number of roster positions, this survival of the fittest environment has extracted tears from many of the biggest and strongest men in the world. I was one of them, but my teammates never knew that. I competed hard every second, driven by the desire to take care of my mother and grandparents, and to hopefully give back to my community. I cried every night, cringing in pain, both mentally and physically exhausted, but came into the training facility each day ready to give my all.

Loose Ball Drill

One of the fi st drills that I participated in during training camp was a drill that combines one-on-one basketball with a loose ball drill. Similar to one-on-one game, this drill is played at half court between two competing players. However, rather than the ball being inbounded at the top of the court, the competition begins at the baseline beneath the basket. Two competing players line up on the baseline as if they are about to race. The coach stands directly beneath the goal, rolls the ball out towards the free throw line, then blows the whistle. At the sound of the whistle, both players race towards the ball, diving, sliding, and colliding into one another with the goal of obtaining possession of the ball, then scoring on the opposing player. It was physical and punishing, and the contact was intense and painful. The object of the game is to get possession, by any means. Quicker players relied on speed, stronger players relied on strength, and longer players leveraged their length to stretch out for the ball. The sound of giant men slamming stomach and chest fi st on the hardwood fl or resembled thunder, and elbows to the ribs and mid-sections seemed more like UFC Fighting than basketball practice. Despite the intensity of this training, I fared well. I was fast, strong, and physical, and competed as if I belonged there. In some instances, I was dominant.

During one round, I was paired with fellow Kansan, Steve Henson. Henson is from McPherson, Kansas, and was a standout player at Kansas State University. I looked up to him when I was young, and now the two of us were on the same team. Though previously a fan, my only current objective was to defeat the 10-year-veteran. I looked over at Henson and thought to myself that there was no way he could beat me running. I had a 40 inch vertical and was a faster sprinter than every player on the team, including the guards. Plus, I have a 7 foot wingspan. My thinking was that I would simply outrun Henson, reach for the ball, and score. Charles O'Bannon had informed me that my speed and athleticism wouldn't be enough, and that I had to learn to utilize my fi st step and body leverage. Suddenly, O'Bannon's advice made sense. Henson and I took off after the ball at full speed. As I expected, I was much faster than Henson, but he had a better angle on the ball, so my speed didn't matter - it appeared that he would win the possession. Most likely, head coach Alvin Gentry was either trying to teach me a lesson or see what I was made of, but it was obvious that he was deliberate in positioning the ball in a manner that gave Henson a clear advantage. Nonetheless, this was a win or go home atmosphere, and every drill, every scrimmage, and every loose ball mattered, so beating the fellow-Kansan was non-negotiable. I was left with no choice but to lower my body, deliberately punch him with my shoulder, and knock him to the ground. I then took two dribbles to the goal, and dunked the ball hard.

In some ways, life itself is like a loose ball drill. Not only are we required to make the most out of what is given to us, but we must also take inventory of our special skills as well as our shortcomings, and leverage our strengths accordingly in rising above obstacles and tough challenges. Though I am at the age where I will never again play professional basketball, I now see myself lined up on life's baseline helping kids chase their dreams while I also chase mine. For the kids that I seek to mentor, the sky is the limit. If they succeed, then my dream of mentoring others to be empowered through my story and my experiences has been fulfilled. In life, Henson may not be on the competing end, but other opposing forces come in various forms. My testimony is that none of these forces are too great to conquer. Lower your shoulder, give it your all, and leave it all on the court in everything you do!

No one is exempt from distractions, pitfalls, and unpleasant encounters. Drugs, gangs, and family problems are common issues that divert some kids and even adults from becoming the best possible versions of themselves. Personal demons come in various other forms as well. In all honestly, my biggest distraction may have been personal accountability, and recognizing this has been critical to my growth and personal fulfillment. Today, I am willing to run hard and fast, lower my shoulder, and knock down the opposing forces that confront me in a manner similar to how I approached the loose ball drill. Through my mentoring, I have empowered kids with similar confidence as means of overcoming their own insecurities. My mentor, and co-author, Dr. Harrison asked me a question once that has always stuck with me. "Who learns the most, an infant or new parents?" This question gave me something to ponder during one of our many intense discussions. I didn't really understand what he was getting at until I started really engaging and working with kids, when I realized that they teach me just as much as I teach them, and inspire me as much as I inspire them. I'm still developing my skills as a mentor and advocate, and in my development, I've learned that mentoring flows in both directions. I can't name all the countless mentors who made sacrifices in order to save me from myself, so I am therefore obligated to pay this mentorship forward.

NBA Teammates

Our team was comprised of all United States players, which is a far cry from the heavy influx of international talent that currently graces the league. Still, our team was certainly as diverse in perspectives and identities as any. In addition to previously mentioned players Joe Dumars, Grant Hill, Charles O'Bannon, Steve Henson, and Christian Laettner, each player was unique in his own right. Many of them had unique interactions and encounters with me.

No.	Player	Pos	Ht	Wt	Birth Date	Exp	College
1	Lindsey Hunter	PG	6-2	170	December 3, 1970	5	Alcorn State, Jackson State University
20	Khalid Reeves	PG	6-3	199	July 15, 1972	4	Arizona
30	Jud Buechler	SF	6-6	220	June 19, 1968	8	Arizona
32	Christian Laettner	PF	6-11	235	August 17, 1969	6	Duke
33	Grant Hill	SF	6-8	225	October 5, 1972	4	Duke
13	Jerome Williams	PF	6-9	206	May 10, 1973	2	Georgetown
52	Don Reid	PF	6-8	250	December 30, 1973	3	Georgetown
12	Steve Henson	PG	5-11	177	February 2, 1968	6	Kansas State
8	Bison Dele	C	6-9	235	April 6, 1969	7	Maryland, Arizona
4	Joe Dumars	SG	6-3	190	May 24, 1963	13	McNeese State University
35	Loy Vaught	PF	6-9	230	February 27, 1968	8	Michigan
31	Mikki Moore	C	6-11	225	November 4, 1975	R	Nebraska
20	Corey Beck	PG	6-1	190	May 27, 1971	2	South Plains College, Arkansas
3	Mark Macon	SG	6-5	185	April 14, 1969	5	Temple
5	Charles O'Bannon	SG	6-5	209	February 22, 1975	1	UCLA
42	Jerry Stackhouse	SG	6-6	218	November 5, 1974	3	UNC
00	Eric Montross	C	7-0	270	September 23, 1971	4	UNC
45	Korleone Young	SF	6-7	213	December 31, 1978	R	

Bison Dele

Perhaps no player on the team was more interesting than Bison Dele. Dele was an individual whose endeavors extended well beyond basketball. Among other things, he was a licensed pilot, a skilled sailor, and an extremely gifted culinary artist.

Dele changed his name from Brian Williams, paying homage to his Native American heritage. It's only fitting that Dele would become a member of the team affectionately known as "The Bad Boys." Though overshadowed by the star power of Jordan and Pippen, Dele, along with former Piston "Bad Boy" Dennis Rodman, were truly the "Bad Boys" of the 1997 Bulls Championship team. From a statistical standpoint, his career average of 11 points and 6 points doesn't just jump off the page. However, true basketball heads know the impact of a 6'10" offensive rebounding artist who was a fie ce defender with a soft touch around the rim. The Pistons understood this very well, and during my rookie season, he became the highest paid Pistons player in the history after signing an unheard of $60 million dollar contract. He didn't disappoint, averaging 16 points and 9 rebounds during our season together, but abruptly retired after just two seasons with Detroit. Passionate about several interests other than basketball, Dele walked away despite leaving a large portion of the money on the table. His personal business and fi ancial manager at the time was Kevin Porter, who is from my hometown, Wichita, Kansas. Porter prided himself on helping Dele leverage his fi ances and investments in a manner that allowed him the fi ancial freedom to walk away from the game with no fi ancial worries.

I will forever be grateful to Dele, who opened his home up to me during my time getting acclimated to living in Detroit. While in training camp, the team paid for me to stay at a local Marriott. Once camp ended, I didn't have an apartment yet, and was more or less given the option of fi ding an apartment or to continue residing at Marriott at my own expense. Dele invited me into his home where I remained for the next two weeks. I would love to have played another season with Dele, but I was released at the end of the season. A couple of years after he retired in 2000, Dele died a mysterious death during a boating excursion. The two of us had developed a close bond, and I was deeply saddened by the news of his death.

Jud Bueschler

Jed Bueschler was a teammate of Bison Dele both in college with the Arizona Wildcats and as a professional with the Chicago Bulls. Since he was a three-time champion with the Bulls, I wanted to pick his brain and learn as much as possible from him, but was never allowed to do so. I was able to develop solid friendships with Christian Laettner and Charles O'Bannon even outside of basketball. Grant and I had a physical altercation during an intense practice session, but he later acknowledged my work ethic and gave me a pair of his signature basketball shoes to symbolize my belonging on the team. Shortly after, Stackhouse gave me two pairs of his signature Fila brand basketball shoes and similar words of encouragement. However, Jud never said a single word to me the entire season, despite the two of us having to compete and guard one another in several practice sessions. He was honestly no match for me in scrimmage settings, so I thought I'd gain his respect by out-playing him every day at practice. I'm not sure what made me think he would be impressed, especially since he had just spent three years playing with Jordan and Pippin. The initiation process of young players having to prove themselves to veterans, combined with everyone competing for limited roster spots creates a competitive and often aloof environment. Despite the nature of this atmosphere, I was able to gain the respect of most of my teammates. However, I outplayed Bueschler in every practice, yet he never acknowledged my existence off he court.

Grant Hill

Of the nearly 541,000 men who play basketball in high school, roughly 18,800 are given the opportunity to compete in college. Each year, approximately 4200 of these players become NBA draft eligible. There are 60 total draft picks, with an average of 8 to 10 spots going to international players. Th s leaves an average of 52 American players each year who are awarded the opportunity to join the fraternity comprised of the world's elite players. Looking at it mathematically, that's barely over 1% of draft eligible players who are actually drafted, with not even one-tenth of one percent of high school players making it to the league. Hence, the odds of winning the lottery and the odds of playing in the NBA are strikingly similar. Therefore, I don't take lightly my tenure of spending countless hours with some of the best players in the world with the Pistons' organization.

Despite everyone being an elite player, and despite being motivated throughout life with the mentality that there is no "I" in team, make no mistake about it – this was Grant Hill's team, and rightfully so. Hill stands at 6'8" and was listed as a small forward, but had the ball-handling ability of a point guard, the scoring instincts of a shooting guard, and the post moves of a power forward. Some of my former teammates may argue, but in my opinion, he could easily have started and dominated at any of these four positions, both offensively and defensively.

Sadly, there is a tendency in Black communities to associate class and sophistication with being soft. Two-parent homes, fi ancial stability, and top-tier education should be celebrated in our culture, but often there is the misbelief that monuments of hard work and overcoming adversity are relics of a pampered life. Being born to a mother who attended a prestigious all female college where she became friends with Hillary Clinton, and a father who graduated from Yale, I imagine Grant has had to deal with this his entire life. While I don't know the backstories of how either of his parents got to those places, I can only imagine that each of their journeys dealt with overcoming racial adversity, systemic oppression, and insurmountable odds. My thinking is that whatever they endured must have required a sense of tenacity and grit that was likely passed down to Grant. Anything about his personal life is mere speculation on my part, but what I do know is that Grant Hill was far from soft, and he made a quick believer of anyone who ever thought this to be the case. He was strong, physical, fiercely competitive, and wasn't afraid to fight if necessary.

Despite all the amazing physical and mental attributes possessed by Hill, I was every bit as athletic, and my team knew it. Did I ever outshine Grant Hill? Of course not. But with my wingspan, I was able to make shots difficult, get my hands on the ball, block shots, and make it difficult for Grant to score by doing things that no one else in the league seemed able to do. The assistant coach for the Pistons at the time, John Hammond, confirmed this, saying:

> "We used to talk about the way in which Korleone Young defended Grant Hill on a daily basis. No one defended Grant Hill in this league as well as Korleone Young."

Hammond now serves as the general manager for the Orlando Magic. Other teammates shared similar sentiments to Hammond. Though he never provided verbal confirmation, the typically well composed and poised Hill occasionally came out of character and displayed visible frustration and anger whenever I had to guard him. One incident took place in New York, as we were preparing to play the Knicks. Grant and I had a small physical altercation. He elbowed me in the back, so I turned around and instinctively fired two quick elbows to his chest and neck, busting his lip open and drawing blood. Shortly after, we grabbed one another and began to scuffle. I was practicing hard but not getting any playing time, so my only option was to train hard, and if there was going to be a scuffle, I had to scuffl just as hard. The team quickly pulled us apart, and Hill held no grudges as expected from a hardnosed competitor such as himself. However, Coach Gentry sent me out of practice, more or less punishing me for fi hting back and being a competitor.

I honestly thought being competitive against Grant would get me some playing time, as did my teammates who would say things like "you really gave Grant problems today young fella," and "keep it up and you gotta get some clock," but it never happened. Instead, it seemed as though I were punished for it. From the bench, I watched Grant torture opposing players who were far less capable of guarding him than I was, knowing full well that I could have made huge contributions to our team. Despite never gaining the respect of my coach, my teammates quickly began recog-nizing my talents.

R-E-S-P-E-C-T

"No one can stop you from scoring in the post!" This is what Charles O'Bannon said to me once I learned how to use my 7'3" wingspan. Most players with my arm length are at least 7 feet tall, so I have ex-tremely long arms for my 6'7" frame. I had gotten to the point where I could score at will in the post as well as pose a threat from the perim-eter, and my team was taking notice – even the legendary Joe Dumas was encouraging. Dumars cheered me on every practice and always taught me something new. Scoring came so easily in scrimmages that during practice, I was eventually even given the nickname "IO" for in-stant offense. Part of my initiation was catering to Dumars. I had to grab his drink, bring him newspapers, and anything else he requested.

Th s was a small price to pay for the knowledge of an NBA champion, 14-year-veteran, and future general manager.

Despite constantly dominating in the post, Coach Gentry would constantly encourage me to stay out of the post. "You're not a power forward young fella!" "You're not big enough to play like that!" I knew I wasn't the best shooter on the team, so I had a drive fi st mentality, but Gentry wanted me to get comfortable taking open shots. Taking his advice, I learned how to score the ball in an assortment of ways, showcasing both midrange prowess and beyond the arc range. One particular practice, I hit five three-point shots in a row from the corner baseline. Keep in mind, I was always on the reserve squad and playing against the stars, yet was still able to score easily. Nonetheless, I never got the opportunity to showcase these skills in games.

Five-Minutes of Game

I fi ally got the nod in a game against the Atlanta Hawks, then later against the Orlando Magic and the Washington Wizards. My entire career playing time was a mere 15 minutes, yet I scored 13 points during my brief stint on the court. I remember each bucket as if they occurred yesterday.

Against Atlanta, I played just under two minutes. I stepped in for Grant to guard Steve Smith. Smith was taller, but I was just as long and as quick, and wanted to prove myself by making it difficult for him on the perimeter. The key with Smith is not to get beat by his hesitation move. Despite everyone in the league knowing this, most players were still incapable of stopping him. For two full minutes, I was able to avoid getting beat by Smith's signature move. Additionally, I scored twice - once on a transition layup and the other, an offensive rebound tip-in.

Just as I was getting warmed up, Coach Gentry was ready for Grant to return, so back to the bench it was for me. All of my teammates acknowledged that I had performed well.

The Orlando game took place during the previously mentioned Bad Boy Reunion game. Former Bad Boy Rick Mahorn served as a guest commentator, and continued to mention my age. "Man, many of us have kids older than Young." Nonetheless, I came in for two minutes once again, and immediately scored four points on Matt Harpring. I had dominated Harpring in the pre-draft camp and had taken it personally that he was selected as a lottery pick, so I went to work on him immediately. Just as the two of us began talking smack back and forth and it appeared that I would be getting the best of him, I was pulled from the game and placed back on the bench. From the bench, I watched Horace Grant eat us alive from the midrange. With my quickness and length, I know for a fact that I could've closed out on Horace and made it difficult for him to score. However, from the bench I could do nothing but sit and watch him score one easy bucket after the next as we suffered a humiliating loss during the homecoming of the Bad Boys legends.

Finally, in the Washington game, I checked in with under fifty seconds remaining on the clock. I shot and made a three-pointer as soon as I hit the floor. Shortly after, I got a rebound and took the ball the dis-tance and made a midrange shot. Since playing time was minimal, I wanted to prove myself within this short spurt, so passing the ball was not an option. Despite scoring five points in under fifty seconds in this game, and 13 points in fifteen total career minutes, I would never again return to the floor for an NBA game. I have no regrets, but I sometimes wish I had been given the opportunity to prove myself.

CHAPTER 13

•

The Legends

A legend is someone who is a step better than great. Th s applies to both sports and life. Greatness can be defi ed by stellar acts and achievements, but legendary is defi ed by accomplishing feats that have never before been accomplished both from a performance and a humanitarian standard. People like the Black astronaut Ron McNair, business mogul Reginald Lewis, and actor Denzel Washington are famous legends, but not all legends are famous. Many of us have people right in our own neighborhoods who are legendary in the way they protect their communities, raise their families, and contribute to society. I've had the pleasure of meeting many legendary individuals both in my community and in the sports world.

Neighborhood Legends: Ernest Corner, Archie Lipscomb, and Jim Harrison

I've always had positive male role models. I've mentioned people like Grandpa Young, Big Henry, Coach Allen, and Sargent Major Payne as men who had a positive impact on my life. I would be remiss not to also mention the men who mentored me in my own neighborhood. I tend to laugh at false biases that assign Black men notions of irresponsibility. I grew up watching proud black men not only take care of their own households, but protect and nurture their entire community. While there are far too many such men to name, three stand out – my next door neighbor, Ernest Corner; my neighbor across the street, Archie Lipscomb; and a half block away, Jim Harrison.

When Mr. Corner passed away last year, it was as if I lost my own father. I grew up playing basketball in his backyard with two of his sons, who were much older than I (Tony and Kevin). In fact, all the older kids in the neighborhood played ball in their backyard, including another neighbor a few houses down, Derrick who was a high school standout for Wichita East in the late 80s. At 7 and 8 years old, I was no match for kids ranging from 16 to 18, but by the time I was 12, I dominated every one of the older kids in the neighborhood. I'm sure none of them will admit this though. Some left for college, others to start careers in the military, and unfortunately, some for prison. Regardless, everyone eventually found their way back to the old neighborhood and found themselves in Corner's backyard.

What I liked most about Mr. Corner was that though he was soft spoken, he was far from soft. He set high expectations for his own four children, as well as for all the kids on the block. When my grandparents passed away, my mother and Aunt Kathy were supportive, but sometimes a young man needs to be consoled by another man. Ernest Corner was always there to support me in that manner.

Mr. Lipscomb passed away several years ago, but much like when Corner died, a piece of me passed away as well. Lipscomb was similar to Corner in the sense that he was married and took care of his family, but different in the sense that he wasn't soft spoken. He had a great sense of humor, and I don't recall ever not seeing a smile on his face. In fact, he always had jokes to tell.

The two youngest of Mr. Lipscomb's four sons (David and Dwayne) were there to watch me grow up. Much like Corner's kids, the Lipscomb boys were like brothers to me. In fact, the entire neighborhood was my extended family. However, that didn't stop me from dunking on each and every one of my play brothers to repay them for how they dogged me out as a little kid. I say that laughingly when in actuality, I realize they were just trying to make me tough. I had the same tough lessons from my cousins Deon, Antoine, and Terry, who were also much older. I was always surrounded by older kids who competed with me as if I were their age.

As a kid, we all admired the Harrison family. From the outside looking in, they were like a television show family. I even looked at them like a Black version of the Kennedy's. They wore nice clothes and had a beautiful home, but that wasn't what made Mr. Harrison legendary in my mind. What made him special was the ownership that he took in our neighborhood. If it was broke, you could take it to him and he would fix it. If a yard needed cut, he didn't call the city, nor did he ask permission to cut it, he just cut it. He picked up trash in the neighborhood, watched over the block, and had tremendous love for his neighbors.

Rather than being called Mr. Harrison, he insisted that the kids in the neighborhood call him Big Jim. If you didn't know him, you might find this amusing. He stands about 5'6" at best. However, his charm, personality, and demeanor are immeasurable. In fact, everything about Mr. Harrison was big. Most importantly, he was big in terms of giving.

Mr. Harrison was a very opinionated and proud Black man who was never short for words of wisdom or trash talk depending on the oc-casion. He still resides in the old neighborhood, I still have a great relationship with him and Mrs. Harrison to this day.

Famous Legends

Knowing the men in my neighborhood, and seeing their shining examples of manhood helped me understand the value of legends, so when I went out into the world, I was able to appreciate legends such as John Thompson and Isiah Thomas. In their own unique ways, Thompson and Thomas reminded me of Corner, Lipscomb, and Harrison.

John Thompson

My decision to skip college and go to the NBA is something that I still feel was the right decision for me at the time. Some criticize me and say that I should have gone to college, but I knew what was right for me and my family, and I stand behind that decision to this day. In this world, everyone will have opinions of what's best for your life. My best advice is to follow your guts, commit hard, and live with the consequences, good or bad, but make it your decision and not that of peer pressure. That said, I don't look back at my life and try to replay all the scenarios of what could've happened better had I gone to college. However, I do wonder what it would have been like to play for the legendary John Thompson and the Georgetown Hoyas.

Coach Thompson was aggressive in recruiting me, and though I hadn't announced it publicly, I had given him a verbal commitment that I would be attending Georgetown. What sold me on Thompson was his honesty. Th s was a trait that the men in my neighborhood possessed, so it was welcoming and familiar. Other coaches made all types of promises, but Thompson did no such thing. In fact, he was upfront in saying that the only promise that he could make was that I wouldn't be starting right away. He told me if I worked hard, I may see some playing time by tournament time, but not to expect it right away. More importantly, he stressed the importance of classwork, expressing that education was equally important as basketball.

Many consider Thompson a legend because he was the first Black coach to ever win an NCAA Championship. For me, his legendary status goes beyond wins and losses. In a lot of ways, Thompson reminded me of Mr. Harrison from the old neighborhood. Both men were brash and cussed a lot. Mr. Harrison had a no-nonsense stare, as he tilted his head upward from his small frame, and looked right into your soul while chewing on the end of an unlit cigar. Coach Thompson never had a cigar in his mouth when we spoke, but used equally expressive language and his demeanor was just as intimidating as Mr. Harrison's. At 6'10", he tilted his head downward when he spoke, with a stare that assured he meant business:

> *Those other clowns are going to promise you a starting position, and promise to get you to the NBA. I can't promise you any of that son, until I see how hard you work and develop. If you want to be a college star or an NBA star, the only person who can promise you that is you. If you outwork everybody else, and get lucky, you may have a chance. All I can promise you is a chance to develop as a player, and the opportunity to get a free education. I want you on the team, but not bad enough to lie to you.*

At 18-years-old, these words didn't mean what they do today. I know so many players who were made false promises by college coaches, so to see a man who stood on firm principles was powerful.

Thompson was a former professional with the Boston Celtics, and playing for one of the most legendary coaches ever in Red Auerbach, backing up the winningest player in the league's history – Bill Russell. I guess the fabric of legends is contagious, and Thompson certainly paid it forward with the development of not just stellar NBA players, but stellar men. College Hall of Fame players like Allen Iverson, Alonzo Mourning, Patrick Ewing, Dikembe Mtumbo, lead the list of players who went on to have exceptional NBA careers, but countless others have gone on to have hall of fame careers outside of basketball. One particular name that stands out in my mind is Michael Jackson, who was drafted to the NBA in 1986, and accepted to Harvard for graduate school the same year. Such was typical based on the type of standards that Thompson set.

Georgetown is a highly rigorous academic institution. Besides having a basketball team that is predominately Black, Georgetown was and still is a predominately White school. Thompson refused to allow his Black players to take academic demands lightly. Seeing how his son, John Thompson III spent his collegiate career at Princeton, it's safe to assume that he set the same standards in his own home as he did for his players.

There are countless traits to admire about Coach Thompson, but nothing more admirable than the lifelong friendships he developed with his players. Players, fans, and friends alike recently shared through social media and interviews, their fondest memories of Thompson, who passed away on August 30, 2020. I can't help but wonder what it may have been like for me to share in those memories. Not so much for basketball development, but more so as a mentor and lifelong friend. I may have never played for Georgetown, but in my heart, I will always be a Hoya. Rest well Big John!

Isiah Thomas

Of all the great players to pass through the Detroit Pistons franchise, most would argue that there are none greater than Isiah Thomas. In fact, by most accounts, Thomas is considered the best Piston ever, and one of the fi y greatest players of all times. Despite expressing personal dislike for Thomas, even Michael Jordan proclaimed him to be one of the best two point guards in NBA history, second only to Magic Johnson. Therefore, to consider Thomas a legend would be an understatement. If there were a basketball Mount Rushmore, Isiah's image would likely be carved in the monumental stone that depicts immortality.

As the leader of the physically tough, mentally intimidating, and championship achieving Bad Boys team that dominated the league in 1989 and 1990, it was only fitting for him to return for the Bad Boys 10 year reunion ceremony. The game was on a Friday (April 2, 1999), but Isiah came to the facility to observe our practice on Thursday. With an almost presidential demeanor, Thomas walked through the gymnasium donning his million dollar smile and displaying the charisma and charm of a Hollywood movie star. Th s was my fi st time seeing him face-to-face. On the outside I had to keep my composure and portray the role of a professional, but on the inside, I was as giddy as a group of teenage girls at a Justin Bieber concert. I was a true fan, and couldn't believe I was seeing Isiah Thomas in the fle h. It was almost surreal watching the larger-than-life celebrity walk through the gymnasium as if moving in slow motion, attracting the unwavering attention of all in attendance. Suddenly, he motioned to one of the trainers for a ball, then called me out for a game of one-on-one in front of the entire team.

"Young fella.... Come on out here and let's see what you got" he shouted out in a laughing manner. I looked around as if he were summoning someone other than myself as the team began chuckling and pointing their fi gers in my direction. Christian Laettner nudged me in the direction of Thomas, and moments later, the two of us began playing. Here I was, a rookie who barely saw any action, about to go head-to-head with one of my childhood favorites and one of the best to ever play the game. I was overwhelmed with fear and nervous energy, but there was no backing down at this point. It felt like yesterday that I was a 10-year-old kid watching Thomas and his teammates shower one another with champagne after winning their second title in 1990. Now at 19, the two of us are standing face-to-face on the same court - the court that he made famous just a few years prior. Players, coaches, trainers, and staff watched eagerly as I checked the ball to Thomas for the fi st possession.

He tried to use his quickness to get around me. He moved from left to right quickly and with fluidity, but I dropped my body low and stretched out to keep him from getting past me on either side. He attempted to drive to my left to get to the basket, but I cut him off. Since he couldn't get to the basket, he spun around and attempted a fl ater shot about 4 feet from the rim. I leaped in the air and swatted the ball so hard that it nearly rolled the complete length of the 94-foot court. Other than that, I don't remember every detail of the game, but I do remember the fi al outcome. After dunking on him several times, blocking several of his shots, and more or less scoring at will, I beat Thomas by a fi al score of 12 to 5. Despite winning the game, I still felt like I lost. Rather than cheering me on, many players and coaches were disappointed that I had humiliated an NBA legend. I've always been told to give my best effort at all times, and to show no mercy regardless the opponent. However, after doing my best against one of the best players in history, I was chastised for not taking it easy. Other than Laettner and O'Bannon, the only other person to celebrate my effort was Thomas himself. He said:

"Young fella… you did exactly what you were supposed to do. Never take it easy on anyone." Then he laughed as he continued talking. "You're a whole lot better than I thought you were. Keep working hard!"

He gave a few more encouraging words, jokingly shared how he beat every single player on the team during his time with the Bad Boys, then patted me on the shoulder and walked away. Thomas was close to 40-years-old, so I won't say that he was at his peak, but I will say that beating a legend of his status felt good regardless of who it may have upset.

CHAPTER 14

•

A Dream Deferred

Harlem by Langston Hughes
What happens to a dream deferred?
Does it dry up like a raisin in the sun? Or
fester like a sore— And then run?
Does it stink like rotten meat? Or crust
and sugar over—like a syrupy sweet?
Maybe it just sags like a heavy load.
Or does it explode?

Have you ever had a dream so real that you woke up lingering in its blissful shadows - somewhere between a state of conscious thought and semi-delusional grandeur, straddling the lines that separate fantasy and reality? Have you experienced lying wide awake, processing colorful collages of subliminal imagery and intangible occurrences as concrete realities? Better yet, have you experienced standing outside of your own body, watching your very image celebrate winning the lottery or other near impossible fantasies, not realizing the truth for several cognizant moments? How about a conversation with a deceased loved one so lifelike that the scent of their skin lingers in your mind moments later?

In his classic poem "Harlem," Langston Hughes eloquently explores possible outcomes of deferred dreams. Though his writing pertains to the social plights of black people in the 1950s, the words are relevant for all people of any era. Since Hughes and I share the commonality of being Black men who spent our childhood in Kansas, I immediately became fond of his work when exposed first at Wichita East, then later at Hargrave. Other than having to learn about the confederate history that symbolizes the state of Virginia, Hargrave Academy provided an enriched educational experience. In fact, they were good about exposing us to literature and pedagogy with cultural relevance, which was surprising and refreshing at the same time.

Despite reading about Hughes in books, it took walking into the most desirable dream imaginable and having it ripped away for me to truly understand the impact of a dream deferred, and the true implication of Hughes poetic words.

I'd be willing to bet that most individuals never have the opportunity to live the life they truly envision for themselves. Of all the things we imagine "being when we grow up," most settle for something less glamourous than the rich and famous fantasies we visualize as kids. I was one of few fortunate souls who didn't have to settle. However, I'm not sure what's worse between never living dreams at all, and having them abruptly taken away. One moment, I was right there – the winner of the lottery – the one who defi d insurmountable odds and reached the peak level of my profession. A year later, I was depressed, alone, living in a foreign country, and wondering what went wrong.

Like most rookies, I was the butt of all jokes, but I was a good sport about it. I never looked at it as anything other than a rites of passage or initiation process, and most of the players embraced me far more than they ever chastised me. None of it was cruel unusual, or malicious. Honestly, it was nothing more than jokes about my age or running errands for veteran players. Simple tasks like getting coffee and newspapers for veteran players when we were on the road was how veterans welcomed young rookies to the team, and to the league.

The environment was highly intense and quite competitive, with older players fully aware that for every new player, an existing player loses his spot. However, veterans were supportive, encouraging, and applauded my consistent growth and development. Unfortunately, one person who never gave such kudos or support was our head coach, Alvin Gentry.

I worked hard every day trying to become better, stronger, and more equipped for NBA competition. I felt I was proving myself. As I stated previously, I was clearly the best defender on our team when it came to guarding Grant Hill. I dominated NBA champion Jud Buschler on a daily basis, and with ease. Christian Laettner and Charles O'Bannon gave me continuous props for my ability to score in the post, and I was celebrated by Jerome Williams for my defensive skills. Kudos from Williams meant a lot to me since he was the player I tried to imitate when it came to defense. I watched him every day in an attempt to duplicate his skill, knowledge, and intensity, which I in turn attempted to apply when guarding Grant in practice. Other players were starting to take notice, encouraging me to keep my head up, feeling certain that I would soon get some playing time. Despite the small altercation mentioned earlier, even Grant was supportive and complimentary of my efforts. For some reason though, no matter what I did, it was never good enough for Coach Gentry.

Doug Collins was the coach when the Pistons drafted me, but the team made a coaching change prior to the season's start, naming Gentry the interim head coach. Initially, I was excited to know that a Black man would be there to hopefully mentor and guide me. I imagined being fostered as a professional the way that Coach Thompson nurtured countless young men at Georgetown. I imagined being developed for the NBA by the type of men I was accustomed to seeing in my neighborhood – men like Archie Lipscomb, Ernest Corner, and Jim Harrison who stopped at nothing when it came to uplifting and encouraging neighborhood kids. I even envisioned traits of Grandpa Young and Big Henry, thinking that Gentry would be hard but fair, challenging me to grow and develop as a player.

Unfortunately for me, he was none of these things, and resembled none of what I expected or knew in other Black men. In fact, he was quite clear in letting it be known that developing me was not his job. I guess I can't blame him. After all, professional basketball is hardnosed and cut throat, and as a new Black coach, I'm sure he was far more concerned with keeping his job than he was supporting a young player.

I have no issue with Gentry showing no interest in my development. In fact, I don't have an issue with him about anything. I do wonder why he refused to give me a chance, even after I developed on my own and proved myself in practice on a daily basis. Whether or not he was verbal in sharing his sentiments of me to other coaches and general managers, his actions said more than enough. Not playing me, then cutting me from the team after one shortened season spoke volumes. Had he only given me a chance, I really believe the outcome would have been drastically different. Instead, when I excelled in the post, he reminded me that I was too small to play in the post, despite my effectiveness offensively and defensively. I demonstrated improvement as a perimeter player, but he would minimize such efforts, attributing great plays and other successes to lucky shots or flukes. And when I relied on midrange scoring, he was quick to inform me that I wouldn't be able to do that in the games, despite doing so when scrimmaging against pros on our team who were just as good and better than most of whom I would face in the league. Any sign of progress, Gentry was quick to shoot down. When I asked what I could do to improve, his responses were limited to vague and meaningless mantras such as "just keep working hard young fella" and "don't give up," but no specific or useful feedback. All the assistants gave me great feedback and confimed that they thought I was ready to play, but Gentry was the boss, and he had no desire to give me that opportunity.

I don't mention Gentry to place blame on him for my less than stellar career accomplishments. While I do think that he could have made a difference, his actions serve as just one of several circumstances that led to my dismissal from the league. Like any other job, career advancement is often determined by someone believing in you, taking a chance on you, and assisting with your professional development. Shortly after being released from the Pistons, I encountered a coach who was willing to offer me all of these things. I have to be totally honest and say that this time, I played a huge role in messing things up.

I ended up with the Philadelphia 76ers, who were coached at the time by Larry Brown. Not only was Brown a legendary coach, but also a personal hero of mine from winning the national championship at the University of Kansas when I was just eight years old. Additionally, he too was an alum of Hargrave Academy.

My workouts were going great, I was holding my own in scrimmages, and every coach on the staff provided favorable feedback. After just weeks, Coach Brown reached out in a way that Gentry never did. He scheduled a one-on-one meeting with me and informed me that I was doing everything right on the court, and that if I continued down this path, while also doing the right things off the court, I would earn a spot on the permanent roster.

I was excited about the possibility of having a coach who would give me a chance, and was ready to celebrate. My chosen method of celebration may have been the kiss of death that sent me packing my bags to never again return to the NBA.

At just 20-years-old, I found myself easily influenced by the glamourous lifestyles enjoyed by some of the more tenured and successful players. Most of these players owned real estate, mutual funds, and other wealth building tools. However, these items don't shine in a manner that capture the eyes of a 20-year-old-kid. Instead, what captured my attention was the expensive jewelry worn by some of my teammates. Diamond earrings, gold necklaces, watches, and rings seemed a walking billboard for a lifestyle symbolic of "making it". I was eager to look and act the part of my wealthy teammates. Though I didn't have access to millions of dollars in disposable income like many of my counterparts, I wanted to be accepted and adored in the manner that they were, so I made the foolish decision to purchase just over $100K worth of jewelry. Overlooking what investing this money could had done for my family, and ignoring my grandmother's warning of "boy don't you buy that jewelry," I felt like I had to have it.

One Saturday night, some of my teammates invited me to hang out at a local nightclub in Philly. I put on all of my new jewelry and rushed to meet the fellas, where I was eager to be adored by the fans. I would be hanging with stars, dressing like stars, and donning the expensive ac-coutrement that comes with the celebrity lifestyle, and I couldn't wait. We decided to leave one establishment and head to another, and I de-cided to stop at an ATM machine. I had several hundred dollars on me, so I'm not sure why I felt the need to stop for more cash. Maybe I fig-ured that flashing money around would compensate for a substandard rookie season. Perhaps I thought that my lack of impressive highlight reels could be overcome by highlighting the perception of an impres-sive lifestyle. Honestly, I can't remember everything that went through my mind at 20. All I know is that buying the jewelry was a terrible idea. Even still, the purchase was nowhere near as bad an idea as wearing $100,000 worth of jewelry at midnight, in Philly, unattended and un-armed.

Without going into great detail of the incident, I was hit in the back of the head with a blunt object, then robbed of my money and jewelry by two unmasked gunmen. I knew they would likely kill me if I didn't cooperate, so without resistance, I allowed them to rob me of the money in my pocket and expensive jewelry that represented the fi al shiny reminder of an NBA career that could have and should have been. More significant than the money and jewelry, and unbeknownst to the robbers – they were also robbing me of an NBA career. This incident and the pay-to-play scandal involving Myron Piggie hit the national news at almost the same time. To the 76ers and to the league, I appeared to be a kid who lacked the decision-making capacity to maintain a career as a professional athlete. The 76ers released me and never again did another team show interest. I thought that I would certainly get another chance, but I never did, even after playing well overseas.

I no longer stress over any of this, and I am thankful that I wasn't severely injured, or even murdered for that matter. What I gained from this experience is far more valuable than the jewelry or even an NBA career. I gained a better knowledge of what is important in life, as well as a story that can motivate any dreamer to not just believe, but to also cherish and nurture that dream with every waking and precious moment of life. Remember to never allow a dream to become deferred even for a brief moment, and to hold your dreams so close to your body that your imagination and your very life are fueled by the same heartbeat.

CHAPTER 15

•

Sweet Psalms in the Hour of Chaos

"Keep the political commentary to yourself, or as someone once said – shut up and dribble."

-- Laura Ingraham – Fox News

The words above are harsh, painful, and downright ignorant, but accurately depict a mentality that represents racism towards Black men in America. Laura Ingraham uttered these cruelties with a sarcastic smirk and malicious demeanor in attempt to insult the intelligence of basketball superstar LeBron James. In the same segment, she implied that James was a "dumb jock" and made fun of a common grammatical error made by fellow NBA star Kevin Durant. Ironically, Ingraham herself made a gross content error in the same segment.

In a country that claims to value multiple perspectives and ideas, the notion of free speech and diversity of thought often seem threatening when coming from Black males. The sad reality is that despite our countless contributions, we are the social population constantly disregarded, devalued, and viewed through a distorted lens of bias and malicious stereotypes. Th s racially motivated frame contains a picture of social injustice that conveniently ignores James's station as a dedicated family man, thoughtful philanthropist, and overseer of a brand that is arguably the best managed in the history of professional sports. Here is a man who invested $40 million dollars towards providing college educations for over 1000 students in the state of Ohio, and an attempt was made to minimize his existence to nothing more than that of an unintelligent person unworthy of a perspective or a voice beyond that of "bouncing a ball." As a Black man and former athlete, I fi d this highly offensive. Similar attacks are common for Black males of every age, and not just in sports.

Sadly, there is a severe gap between who we truly are and what many choose to see. Take for example former Utah Jazz guard and all-time NBA assist leader John Stockton. Stockton never hired an agent to negotiate his contracts, instead dealing face-to-face with previous Utah Jazz owner Larry Miller. Though unheard of, this move was categorized as "leadership" and "gutsy" when made by Stockton (who is White), but when James opted to move in a similar manner; assembling business savvy, highly competent, and trustworthy Black friends to manage his rapidly growing brand, the sentiment was that he was making a huge mistake. The unspoken assumption was that there was no way that these young Black men with no college degrees would be able to effectively manage the LeBron James brand. Since that time, LeBron and his associates have developed a business model that is studied, imitated, admired, and envied by his peers.

If doubting the competency of LeBron and his staff were not insulting enough, what was even more offensive were actions that occurred after their success. Without going into great detail, there have since been attempts to prohibit gifted Black businessmen from operating in this space. LeBron's agent, Rich Paul has become one of the most competent professionals in the fi ld, and an attempt to implement a rule that is unoffi ally called the "Rich Paul Rule" demonstrates the exact sentiment of Ingraham's racially insensitive quote. Although the rule was reversed, it would have prohibited agents like Paul from representing some of the top sports talent in the world without fi st obtaining a college degree.

College degrees are certainly worthwhile and even necessary for many individuals, but based on Paul's success, I would venture to guess that a degree is not necessary for what he provides for LeBron. Though I've never attended college, I do place high value on education. However, I don't imagine there is a class that teaches how to manage a billion dollar sports brand for a celebrity athlete. Th s is an education that can only be realized at the crossroads where preparation and opportunity intersect.

LeBron is considered the king for what he does on the court, but his off- he-court maneuvers are just as impressive. The same way that he sees the entire court and knows what individuals are in best position to score, he has the ability to analyze business talent in the same manner, and put the right people in the right positions accordingly. Th s is quite impressive and in no way represents a "dumb jock" who is only good for "dribbling a ball."

Another example of unfair biases in sports can be seen by examining the Kobe Bryant rape allegation in comparison to the sexual misconduct allegation of Ben Roethlisberger. While I would never minimize the heinous nature of sexual misconduct, we are told that we live in a country where we are innocent until proven guilty. I think I speak for many Black men throughout the nation when I say that our reality better resembles "guilty until proven innocent," but more than a sentiment, there are numerous court cases and examples that support this uncomfortable belief. The disparities between how Kobe's case was handled and that of Ben's is one example of such. Kobe suffered public crucifixi n of character prior to adequate legal exploration, while Ben's case was more or less brushed over despite admitting to the accusation. Countless other examples exist showing the disparities between Black athletes and our White counterparts, but this exists outside sports as well. Black men in America are continually targeted by biases that say we are hypersexual, unintelligent, and violent.

When we (Black men) are "dribbling balls" or dancing or entertaining, everyone is happy; but when we begin to demonstrate intellectual and business prowess, people tend to get nervous. Th s is the simple yet sickening reality of systemic racism. Though we can eat in the same restaurants and attend the same schools, segregation is still a factor. Essentially, this represents an existence of encountering ostensibly segregated experiences within physically desegregated spaces. The disparity between White and Black rules creates double standards just as intense as double overtime, and as illegitimate as double dribbling.

Similar ideas form the basis for mental attacks against Black boys in K-12 schools, and Black men who are physically attacked by law enforcement. It's saddening to know that even fame and wealth fail to provide protection from these destructive realities. However, I'm thankful for people like James, who uses his status to challenge these harmful narratives. I don't have millions of dollars or a global platform, but it doesn't take all that. I've learned fisthand from people like Grandpa Young, Big Henry, Coach Allen, Coach Keates, and some of the neighborhood fathers that Black men can and do make a difference in their communities and in the world. Similar to Lebron's story, so many Black men are living examples of excellence throughout every facet of society.

Racism exists throughout the world, but it's different in the United States. It took my leaving the country to realize that biases depicting us as savage and menace creatures is not as common in other countries. In fact, in many countries, people are disturbed by how Black people are treated and viewed in America. I played in Australia, Russia, Israel, China, and Italy, and never did I experience wrongful traffi stops or women clinching their purses in elevators. There were no news reporters suggesting that Black athletes "shut up and dribble," nor were there uprisings of White supremacist groups. I'm not saying that race didn't play a role, but race was much less signifi ant in other parts of the world. Some people loved Americans and others didn't, but whether we were loved or hated, we were typically viewed as Americans – not Black Americans. The only country that rivaled the United States in terms of racism towards Blacks was Israel. Ghettos in the United States are like country clubs in comparison to ghettos of Israel. These are the poorest and most dangerous neighborhoods I have ever seen, and most of the poverty and despair is based on racial injustice towards darker people.

My fi st international stop was Australia in the city of Canberra, the capital city. Being from Wichita, it was exciting to play for former Wichita State Shocker star Cal Bruton, who was my head coach in Australia. Bruton went undrafted in in the 1976 NBA draft despite being one of the top guards in the country. I assume his height was a factor for no team giving him a chance, which is too bad. I am certain that Bruton could have been a major contributor despite standing just 5'9" tall. He went on to have an amazing career in Australia, and as fate would have it, he became my coach for a season where I was predicted to become the league MVP. After dominating the preseason in every statistical category, I suffered a ruptured Achilles in the fi st regular season game and had to miss the remainder of the season.

I went to China to help launch a brand new league that still exists and is quite successful. I was one of the fi st Americans to play in China, and was treated amazingly well during my five-year tenure there. I played for three teams in China, and was the only American on my team each season. I had a great career in China, leading the league in scoring, rebounds, and blocks every season while there, including setting the single-game scoring record of 58 points.

Other than Italy and Russia, China was as competitive as any country I have played in. Besides basketball, it was fascinating to learn customs and traditions of other countries. I never became fluent in any language besides English, but learning various words and basic conversational skills were amazing experiences. Living the life of an international citizen provided a world education that four years of college could not have provided. Nothing against textbook learning, but living abroad provides education in ways one cannot imagine.

Despite living abroad, learning customs, and emerging as an international citizen, and even making large sums of money, I was never fully happy. My career average overseas was just under 30 points per game, with double digit rebounds and multiple blocks. However, being homesick and unable to play in front of friends and family typically outweighed the success I was having.

Since the NBA has developed its own minor league, there no longer exists a need for the CBA. During my professional tenure, the CBA (Continental Basketball Association) served as an unoffi al farm system that developed future NBA talent. I played for two separate teams in the CBA, both with legendary coaches. In Illinois, my coach was former Oklahoma University All- American and Chicago Bulls player Stacy King. In Richmond, Virginia, my coach was 7 foot All-American and former professional Ralph Sampson. I led the CBA in blocked shots, while remaining in the top ten scorers, averaging 27 points per game.

Playing in the CBA may have lessened my homesickness, but it didn't lessen my depression. Looking back at it, I suppose I should have been grateful. After all, I was fortunate to play a game that I loved, and made a great living doing so. However, I wanted to return to the NBA. As the game rapidly becomes an international sport, global competition keeps gets better and better. The growing number of international players doing well in the NBA is evidence that some leagues nearly mimic the NBA in terms of competitiveness and talent. Still, there is nothing quite like the experience of being an NBA player. I can't explain exactly why, but at times, it was more fulfilling to sit on the bench in Detroit than it was to be a featured superstar in other leagues.

Nonetheless, while in the CBA, reality sat in a manner that captures the sentiment of words shared by the late Christopher Wallace (Notorious B.I.G.). In the song "Juicy," the hip-hop legend refl cts upon his childhood poverty stating "birthdays was the worst days." I was fortunate to never have dealt with extreme poverty as a child, but as a professional athlete still desiring to make an impact, every birthday became less celebratory and more a reminder of the inevitable outcome against time – the opponent that has never been defeated. I dominated every league I played in, but with each new draft class, prospects from the previous year become less attractive, and yesterday's rising stars commonly become today's "has-beens". Images of greatness easily fade away, and like weathered photographs, depictions of what once was become undecipherable relics of irrelevance. Hence, the desire for fortune and fame was never the source of my depression. Instead, it was the desire to prove myself to the world that I was worthy of an NBA career, but I was never again given opportunity to do so. To put it into a different perspective, imagine feeling as dispensable as a piece of gum that was once sweet and tasty, but has suddenly lost its flavor.

With so many talented players throughout the nation competing for a finite number of NBA roster spots, teams and fans alike are constantly seeking new faces, or like the previously mentioned gum analogy – new flavors. But sports is not the only avenue where competition exists in this manner. In fact, the same can be said for engineers, accountants, sales professionals, and every other career imaginable. No matter how good you may be in a certain position or career, the fact stands that we are all replaceable, and new talent continues to funnel through the pipeline of every industry. Therefore, my challenge to you is to remember that time is the one commodity that cannot be replaced. Lost homes can be rebuilt and lost money can be re-earned, but not a second of time can be relived. Seize every opportunity as if it may be your last, because as my story illustrates – it may very well be.

CHAPTER 16

•

Welcome to the Ghetto

I could remember being whipped in class
and if I didn't pass mama whipped
my ass.
Was it my fault, papa didn't plan it out?
Broke out left me to be the man of the
house.

Tupac Shakur

Those who know me know that I am affectionate when I speak of my old neighborhood. As I've grown older, I've found this to become common with most Black folks. Years of systemic oppression have made land ownership a scarce and rare commodity among African American populations, so our desire for ownership sometimes manifests through expressing loyalty to certain neighborhoods, blocks, housing additions, and geographic sections. Hip-hop music has played a tremendous role in showcasing this tendency globally. Energetic celebrations of Compton, California by recording artists such as N.W.A and DJ Quik; the rapper Scarface paying homage to Houston's infamous fi h ward; New York artists mentioning specific boroughs and housing additions; and countless other examples demonstrate the fact that neighborhoods are as much a part of who we are as our family names, occupations, and religious affiliations.

We pay reverence to our neighborhoods for the special role they play in our upbringing, but every moment isn't pleasant. While some memories are as sweet as the taste of honey suckle that grows wild on inner-city vines, others are the gravel and blood on the tongues of young boys who fall face fi st on asphalt pavement. Bicycle accidents, tackle football games, and neighborhood fist fi hts provide the battle scars that are common rites of passage for kids coming from predominately Black neighborhoods, but most of these events are far too fond to associate with sustainable despair. The scrapes and blemishes of boyhood are usually temporary. Small setbacks that can be easily kissed away by a loving mother, or washed away by the baptismal of summer sweat beneath smoldering sunlight. And for those moments that can't be fi ed by a tender kiss or fun times with friends, Red Kool-Aid typically does the trick. Funny enough, Kool-Aid has never branded a flavor by such a name as "Red" but in urban communities where ownership is scarce, we even create our own language. As a result, "Red" has been the Kool-Aid flavor of choice for decades.

Of course, there are bitter memories that are less temporary and far less desirable than the simple setbacks previously mentioned. Often, the sounds of gunshots resonate through the shadows of dark nights in syncopation with ghetto lullabies sung by worried mothers – sometimes in homes where fathers are unseen and other times unknown, incarcerated, or intoxicated. Cracked pavement and crack pipes are reminders of broken dreams and broken promises that refl ct tales of two cities, yet with love we embrace one another with upside down palms exchanging "Five on the black side". Meanwhile, pick any five blocks in White neighborhoods, and I guarantee they are equipped with far better resources than any "five on the Black side." Helicopters and sirens form the soundtrack for a reality show that continuously monitors the movements of African American residents with the commonality of moons and suns trading places, and the regularity of darkness making way for light. Bad news of murders and violence travels through grapevines and gossip channels with the weight of gravity, but on local news, Black lives seem less signifi ant than local sports, often taking backseat to Wichita State basketball highlights that begin with "How 'bout those Shockers". Then there is the mass incarceration of Black men from urban neighborhoods throughout the nation.

My NBA career begins and ends with stories that refl ct these realities, starting with the night of my NBA draft in 1998. I realize there are those who truly believe that policing is consistent regardless of ethnicity, but this is a blatantly false assumption. The writer of my book (Dr. Harrison) is a lifelong family friend and at the time, he and his dad were the owners of the bar where my family opted to have my NBA draft party. Two years prior, his younger brother had been arrested on drug conspiracy charges that the state of Kansas opted to place on WOP (Without Prejudice). Federal authorities had two years to prosecute the charges federally, and opted to do so in month 23 of the 24 month window. From what I understand, the warrant for his arrest was issued over a week prior to draft night. However, we had advertised heavily for the event, and it was obvious that the Wichita Police Department was more interested in making an abrupt scene than they were upholding the law. In an attempt to lessen any unnecessary commotion, my friend not only stayed home, but called the police department to inform them that he was aware of the warrant and that he would be home waiting to surrender to authorities with no resistance. Of course, this was far too civil and failed to garner the attention these officers were seeking. Midway through the draft party, a couple of dozen officers stormed into the bar with flashlights pointing in faces and with guns drawn.

Despite my troubled friend's name not being on the lease, the sergeant demanded that he come to the bar, and stated that they wouldn't leave until he did, despite knowing that he was at his home waiting to be arrested. I'm not sure that it's legal to demand the presence of a person in a place that is neither their residence nor place of business. It's certainly unethical to focus more on making a massive scene than simply "protecting and serving" in the most simple and efficient manner. Nonetheless, this happened on the night of my draft. One of the highest moments of my life was compromised by the harsh reminder of biased policing, racial profiling, and a general sense of entitlement beyond what is authorized by the badge. Profiling of this nature has become so common in Black communities that no one was even alarmed by the blatantly disrespectful and highly inappropriate protocol exercised by these offic s.

Fast forward 13 years, just five years after retiring from overseas competition, and I found myself in another undesirable situation in 2011. In a sense, these two events would symbolize a career that began and ended with realities described by Aretha Franklin as "living in a world of ghetto life." But this time the consequences were far more life threatening. To make a long story short, I was attending a birthday party at a home that would later be targeted for potential robbery. There was a knock at the door, and I opened it expecting nothing more than additional party guests. Immediately, several shots were fi ed, with me and another former NBA player both barely escaping the house despite being pursued by two armed gunmen. Unfortunately, amidst the commotion there was a casualty. One of the gunmen accidentally shot and killed his accomplice, and was charged for the murder. My NBA career began with me being in the middle of police misconduct in Wichita; a couple years later I was robbed at gunpoint at an ATM machine in Philly; and fi ally, the end of my career was accentuated by an incident that could have cost me my life, and did result in my witnessing a murder. It's important to understand that these types of incidents are not uncommon. I traveled the world, yet my home was more racist than most of the countries I had visited abroad, and my neighborhood more dangerous.

I don't blame ghetto life for my shortfalls as an NBA player, or even as a man for that matter. The ghetto is as much a state of mind as it is a physical location, and one of my failures was not allowing my mindset to change. Thus, the ghetto was there to send me off as I left to become a professional; was there to greet me in Philly; and was waiting for me upon my return to Wichita. Our demons lie within us, and have the tendency to follow us around the world and back if we aren't careful. My advice to anyone reading this who has endured similar struggles is simple - use my story to be better than I have ever been. I would love to have the chance to go back and give this information to the 18-year-old Korleone Young, but I have to admit – the 41-year-old Korleone has benefited from these self-refl ctions as well. Hopefully, someone reading this will also benefit. Th ough it all I have lost money, a career, cars, jewelry, and other material possessions. There were even times that I felt like I had lost my mind. Still and yet, I have weathered life's toughest storms, and like the old church song declares, I have lived to "tell the story of how I've overcome." I have dealt with depression, alcoholism, and excessive usage of marijuana, but these distractions never worked, and often made things worse - but as the same gospel song referenced above states, "we will understand it better, by and by." It was when I decided to live my remaining days with purpose that I started to have a better perspective of life, its meaning, and my personal purpose.

Understanding purpose is difficult for some people. At least it certainly was for me. In fact, this is something I am still fi e tuning, which is okay – we are all a work in progress. My fi st step was understanding that the purpose I designed for myself may not be the one that was designed for me. I heard a quote that says "if you want to make God laugh, tell him your plans." Being a famous and wealthy athlete was my plan, and there are things I could have done differently to better the odds. Still, this may not have been my life's divine plan.

Purpose can be better understood by looking at the life of Greek philosopher Diogenes who believed in virtue as an action rather than theory. He traveled by foot, carrying a lamp in broad daylight, claiming to be in search of men with honesty and virtue. To me this symbolizes the purpose of taking light to dark places, not in the sense of light and darkness as physical properties. But as forces that differentiate qualities such as good and evil; love and hate; altruism and selfishness; and knowledge and ignorance.

My challenge to you is to identify the light that you are charged with taking to dark places. Perhaps it's a high aptitude for math and science, or eloquent speaking and writing skills. Maybe you are a great motivator or leader. Whatever it is, God didn't design you to play it small. All of us are ordained with a calling on our life to shine our light in places of darkness. Strangely, the darkness of my past has become the light of my future. My mistakes, my shortcomings, my fears, and my insecurities have become the tools that I now use to inspire myself and others. It took a great deal of soul searching for me to get to this point, and being honest with myself about things that I avoided facing for years. However, once I became able to look inward rather than outward, I became free from my own transgressions.

All that said, purpose for me is simple. We all make mistakes, and God knows that I am the rule rather than the exception. However, most mistakes can be rectified if we are humble and thoughtful. In fact, rather than being ashamed of our past failures, they should be used as life lessons, character building mechanisms, and teaching tools for others. It is my hope that both my trials and triumphs are inspirational for anyone needing to know that it is never too late to reclaim a life with purpose.

Every block of stone has a statue inside it and it is the task of the sculptor to discover it. I saw the angel in the marble and carved until I set him free.

Michelangelo - referencing to the statue of David

CHAPTER 17

•

Arc of Redemption – Part One

A redemptive arc is a storytelling mechanism that introduces a character who is severely flawed. In many stories, the flawed character is even evil or destructive to themselves and to others. By the end of the story, the flawed character corrects their most noticeable flaws, essentially transforming from villain to hero. I don't consider myself a massive failure, but writers around the country have depicted otherwise, so the antihero version of Korleone Young has already been created. Despite a great career overseas, I have been the subject of scrutiny in newsprint, internet blogs, and barbershop conversations throughout the country. I'm not angry about any of this. I've had my fair share of mess ups, so my character flaws often fed right into these otherwise defic t-informed narratives. I'll speak to each of these later, but my biggest mistakes include a car accident that left a teammate severely injured; a less than ideal relationship with my children; and a trail of intimate relationships that were unhealthy and unfulfilling for both parties.

Like any arc of redemption, mine requires first recognizing my personal flaws, being intentional about overcoming them, and being an example for others who have experienced similar battles with personal demons. Of course, overcoming our demons is far easier to say than to do, but I have developed a process that I believe could work for others as it has for me. I've never wanted to hurt others, but my personal demons have been a source of pain, both physical and mental, for people I have truly cared about. As mentioned before, my teammate, my girlfriends, and my children have all suffered with me as I have battled with the isolation and depression of what I once perceived as failure. I now perceive my life as success, because my story can be used to inspire others. It is my hope to once again work for the NBA in the capacity of mentoring young players on ways to avoid some of the pitfalls that I am quite familiar with. Before diving into the process I used to begin turning my life around, I'd like to first share some thoughts on personal demons.

Strikingly similar to converging winds, demons appear suddenly and from various directions. At times they can be ice cold and unexpected like the heartless reality of frozen aspirations or stifled desires. At other times, humid and dense like the sunbaked earth where slave ancestors dwelled under constant racial terror. Unlike the familial warmth of a mother's love, our demons dehydrate our imaginations and starve our fondest desires – dream killers that wither away pleasant fantasies like flowers un-watered, ideas un-nurtured, and potential unfulfilled.

Despite outward expressions of smiling faces, positive vibes, and other misleading facades, demons connect to the cores of our souls, and like dark secrets, move in synchrony with each breath and heartbeat.

The falling of every tear and the silence of furtive whispers carry their voices - silent but deadly – unassuming yet lethal – distant yet near.

No matter how swiftly we run or the distance of our travels, our demons look us in the eyes each morning as mirror refl ctions that stare back – diluted versions of ourselves. Often disguised by name-brand accoutrement and cosmetic coverings, we habitually endure the arduous daily task of masking our deepest fears and insecurities beneath fraudulent and exaggerated interpretations of reality.

As our demons remind us of the mistakes that discourage us from dreaming, and deter us from forgiving ourselves for sins of the past, they create depressive symptoms that in turn, cause our hearts to grow angry and cold. Deeper still, our demons convince us that they can be escaped by navigating yellow brick roads and proverbial underground railroads, seeking answers that were always within us, and freedoms from chains that restrict our minds despite the illusion of physical bodies that are devoid of constraint. Hence, we can leave relationships, jobs, and even countries, but our demons never leave because they don't just reside within us – they are us. They travel as we travel – run as we run – and when we attempt to hide from them, they are right there hiding with us. Hiding from the truth, hiding from reality, and hiding from our solutions to living a life with purpose.

That said, let me share a speech that my mentor and co-writer Dr. Harrison shared with me. I'm not sure where he heard it, but he started the conversation by bringing attention to the fact that I have done quite a bit of air travel, so he asked me what I remembered about flying in airplanes. I stammered around for a second, speaking about turbulence on international fli hts, lost luggage, and being jetlagged. He smiled, and continued the conversation, this time asking "what do you remember about the emergency procedures that are shared over the intercom?" After going back-and-forth, he finally led me to the instructions that say "Be sure to put the mask on before helping others." I never thought about it until he put it into perspective, but we really can't save others until we first save ourselves – sometimes even from ourselves.

To save myself, I had to first face some hard to swallow truths about myself. Looking in the mirror and being honest with ourselves is a difficult thing to do, and in previous years I was incapable of doing so. With age and maturity though, we learn to process information from a wiser and broader perspective. I would never challenge you to take this difficult leap unless I had already begun this journey myself. Here are some of the truths that I have accepted, as the next chapter of my life will involve moving past my previous shortcomings, and walking in the purpose mentioned in the previous chapter:

TRUTH ONE

I don't have the best of relationships with my children, but it's not too late for me and it's not too late for you to repair severed and damaged affiliations and bonds…

In 2000, almost two years after being cut from the Pistons, my oldest daughter was born. Though I was no longer receiving NBA income, my child support amount was based on my salary with the Pistons. I fought this for years, but it took close to 14 years to get this corrected and have my support payments aligned with my true income. With the substantial decrease in pay, I struggled to pay as much of the $2000 per month as I could while playing abroad. After returning from overseas,

I could no longer afford to pay it, so before long, I was severely in arrears.

Similar frustrations were present in relationships with my other children. The combination of fi ancial ruin, depression, and feelings of failure were the excuses that I gave myself for modeling the same example of fatherhood that Juan Johnson had set for me. Meanwhile, part of my growth is to refrain from making excuses, and instead make strides in the right direction. I am currently working with an attorney to make reasonable payments to get this issue resolved. While I know it is a process that will take time, I am also reaching out and making attempts to slowly build relationships with my children. Additionally, as men we are obligated to fi d ways to break destructive cycles, not mimic them. I realize now that I should have never allowed my frustrations and personal inadequacies to interfere with building relationships with my kids. However, we cannot un-spill milk once it's spilled, so there is no value in dwelling on the past. What is within our power, is to clean up life's spills. We do this by recognizing that we are not perfect and being willing to admit our mess-ups; we also do this by rebuilding damaged relationships and accepting responsibility. Lastly, even when it is hard, we must hold ourselves accountable.

My challenge to anyone needing to mend a broken relationship is to take the fi st step and reach out no matter how difficult it may be. Pick up the phone, write a letter, send a text, or whatever it takes to get the conversation started, and don't be ashamed to say "I'm Sorry." Just know that our time on earth is far too limited to carry grudges or to miss opportunities to share precious moments and words with those whom we love. I'm a fi m believer that love can heal major differences, so love hard!

TRUTH TWO

Some of my personal decisions have caused me to squander away substantial financial resources. We can re-earn lost money and rebuild lost homes, but we cannot regain time. I have learned to no longer take time for granted and to treat every second as if it were gold…

When I announced that I would be entering the draft, NIKE had immediately become interested in an endorsement deal. There was even talk about a possible sneaker using my initials, which would have been perfect considering that my full name Suntino Korleone Young spells SKY. The Nike SKY would have made an excellent name for an athletic shoe that promotes a game that is often played above the rim.

The deal was pretty simple. I already had a relationship with NIKE from my days on the AAU circuit, so all I needed to do was sign the contract and walk away with a $500,000 check. I was just 18 and had no clue how these business dealings worked, so I trusted other people to handle my business. "You are worth no less than $40 to $60 million dollars Korleone" is the advice I was given, despite never stepping foot on an NBA court. Obviously, this was poor advice looking back at it.

After an injury that kept me from playing in the McDonald's All-American game, measuring at 6'7" rather than 6'8", and rumors of the pay-to-play allegations mentioned in an earlier chapter, my stock dropped from being a middle fi st-round pick, to being projected anywhere between late fi st round and middle second-round, despite having excellent workouts. As we continued to go back-and-forth with Nike, the offer continued to dwindle. By the time I finally signed, they had reduced the initial offer to just $50,000 and the possibility of the signature shoe was no longer on the table.

As you read this, you may have a tendency to feel sorry for me based on missing out on the opportunity to help my family or support my kids with the money that I let slip away. If so, I ask you not to do that – I've already done it, and it does no good. I spent over a decade so stressed out about the money and opportunities that slipped away, to the point that I missed out on chances to pursue new opportunities. With my camps and youth leagues, speaking engagements, and other ventures, I am working towards rebuilding my brand. What I learned is that we cannot continue to beat ourselves over the head about lost opportunities. Instead, we must learn from our mistakes, position ourselves for new opportunities, then make better choices as we pursue new new dreams, and new goals.

TRUTH THREE

I am learning to turn my tests into my testimonies, but it took first understanding the true meaning of pain. Secondly, it took understanding that I have been hurt, and I have hurt others...

When I was a child, physical pain was the extent of my understanding of hurt. I knew what emotional discomfort felt like, and I knew what it felt like to be let down. Thi gs like not having a relationship with my father and being too tall to participate in Biddy Basketball were early experiences that sometimes saddened and confused me, but they didn't physically hurt, so I didn't associate them with pain. As kids, we feel things intuitively that we don't always have the language to speak to.

By high school, I had developed the cognitive maturity to understand that pain could manifest as agony and suffering beyond physical distress. Despite having a better understanding of emotional, psychological, and mental anguish, my experiences with non-physical pain were limited to encounters with low stakes. Not winning a state title at East High or being suspended for games seemed devastating until I actually encountered a truly traumatic experience. During my junior year of high school, a close friend was struck by lightning and died. I will always be competitive and passionate about winning, but for the fi st time, I recognized greater meaning in life than the things that I had initially placed optimal value on.

As an adult, I have experienced the deaths of two grandparents, a mother, Big Henry, my Aunt Imo, my older cousin Beverly, and several friends and family members, including one of my closest friends, Freddie Tresvant. I have also watched helplessly as close acquaintances have dealt with incarceration, addiction, and various other perils that have ravaged Black communities and Black families. In addition to witnessing pain that others have gone through, my personal pain was becoming more intense as my mother and grandparents became less responsible for guiding and protecting me, and manhood fell directly upon my shoulders.

I must admit, I wasn't prepared and made tremendous mistakes, personally and professionally. Some of these have been hurtful to me, and some have caused physical and mental pain to others. You may have read about some of these incidents, including an automobile accident in Australia that left a teammate injured. No longer young and sheltered, my experiences of letting others down suddenly had greater risks than forgetting to take out the trash or feed the dog. Disappointing others suddenly had greater consequences than bringing home a bad grade or forgetting my mother's birthday. Previously, I had my grandparents and mom to look out for my personal needs, and for everything else there were my older cousins Deon, Antoine, and Terry. Th s was my village and they always had the right answers. However, there comes a time that a man is required to have his own answers.

In case you want to give me the excuse that I was 18 and thrust into manhood too quickly, save it. I too gave myself that excuse, but that was long ago. The reality is that most of my major mistakes took place well after the age of 18. In this journey called life, we sometimes let ourselves down as well as others. I recognize this and want to use my mistakes as stepping stones towards greatness as I continue writing life's next chapter. Life is very similar to basketball. You have to practice, prepare, and stay game ready as each day presents new challenges and new opportunities, some expected and others unexpected. Th ough being transparent about both my successes and failures, I plan to empower myself and others with a blueprint that prepares them to treat every day like game day. For me, this involves continuing to work with kids with everything from literacy programs, basketball development clinics, motivational speaking, and mentoring. It is my hope to once again do business with the NBA, working with young players as part of rookie orientation and ongoing professional off-c urt development. My life's journey is a journal of highs that rival the wildest dreams of many, and lows that I would never wish on anyone. I therefore know what it takes to succeed, and I know how it feels to fail. More importantly, failure is part of life, but from my experiences, I know what it takes to minimize its probability, and I know how to rebound from failure and get back on the track to greatness. Besides, who better to consult with the new generation of young NBA stars than the man who, as previously stated, many attribute professional basketball's "One and

Done" rule to?" In case you forgot who I am, allow me to reintroduce myself…

With the 40th pick of the 1998 NBA draft, the Detroit Pistons select, 18-year-old Korleone Young, a 6'7" small forward from Wichita, Kansas…

And with the 1st pick of the 2020 draft, a life with purpose and direction selects, 41-year-old Korleone Young; still 6'7" and still from Wichita, Kansas. The difference is that he no longer plays forward – now he is moving forward!!

CHAPTER 18

•

Arc of Redemption - Part Two Companion Guide and Summary

My three truths explain acknowledgement of my personal demons, and challenging others to do the same. Th s section provides an approach to minimizing our demons, and requires five steps that are simply stated yet complex in their execution. These must be approached in the same manner and with the same precision as an artist crafting a masterpiece. Like Michelangelo's approach to creating the renowned Statue of David, we must develop the ability to recognize the masterpiece that resides within each of us - far beneath the baggage that disguises the core of who we are. Thus, we must continue chipping away the excess until we reach a conception that is true to form with the beautiful and artistic being that God created. Th ough chipping away shortcomings and insecurities; peeling back multiple layers of emotional and psychological trauma; carving away failures and past mistakes; and discarding the need to be validated by others, I have discovered a simplistic and organic version of who I truly am. Like a masterfully created sculpture or breathtaking self-portrait, I believe that we are all capable of tapping back into our core characteristics, redefini g who we are, and recognizing that we were designed to pursue and achieve endless possibilities. I can't repeat enough times that I am far from perfect, and still a work in progress, but balancing the art of intuition with the science of intentionality has helped me make tremendous strides towards improving myself, forgiving myself, seeking forgiveness from others, and redeeming myself. Here are the steps that have assisted me in crafting my redemptive arc:

Finding the Masterpiece within – 5 Careful Steps

1. It is never too late to:
    a. Dream
    b. Reinvent and Recreate Yourself
2. Admit Fault:
    a. Be truthful to yourself and to others
    b. Reach out and apologize and repair damaged relationships
3. Forgive Others:
    a. If you expect others to forgive you, you have to forgive as well. We all deserve a second chance
4. Forgive Yourself
    a. We are all human and therefore all make mistakes.
    b. We can't erase past mistakes, but we can be intentional about not repeating the same patterns of mistakes.

- c. When we fail to forgive ourselves we punish ourselves and others.
5. Masterpiece Crafting
    a. We have the power and ability to craft a masterpiece in our own image.
    b. We do this by reinvesting in relationships, using our mistakes to empower others, and advocating and mentoring as means of giving back to our communities.
    c. We also do this by visualizing our best life and setting realistic goals that will help us get there. My goal is to work with youth and young adults, and use my story to empower them in sports and in life. I challenge you to write out your goals and set a plan in motion today!

I am Korleone Young, and this is my story…

www.ingramcontent.com/pod-product-compliance
Lightning Source LLC
Chambersburg PA
CBHW051057160426
43193CB00010B/1227